Images of Women in Film
The War Years, 1941-1945

Studies in
American History and Culture, No. 21

Robert Berkhofer, Series Editor

Director of American Culture Programs
and Richard Hudson Research Professor of History
The University of Michigan

Other Titles in This Series

Images of Women in Film

The War Years, 1941-1945

by
M. Joyce Baker

umi
RESEARCH PRESS

Produced and distributed by
UMI Research Press
an imprint of
University Microfilms International
Ann Arbor, Michigan 48106

Library of Congress Cataloging in Publication Data

Baker, Melva Joyce.
    Images of women in film.

    (Studies in American history and culture ; no. 21)
    Originally presented as the author's thesis, University
of California, Santa Barbara, 1978.
    Bibliography: p.
    Includes index.
    1. Women in moving-pictures. 2. World War, 1939-
1945—Moving-pictures and the war. 3. Moving-pictures
—United States. I. Title. II. Series.

PN1995.9.W6B3 1980   791.43'09'09352042   80-39795
ISBN 0-8357-1153-6

Contents

List of Plates
Following page 82

Preface

My interest in the images of women in popular feature movies of the World War II years grew from my concern with the history of American women rather than from a fascination for Hollywood products of the early 1940s. Although watching old films on television or going to the movies was a pleasurable entertainment, I had seldom applied the analytical tools of the historical profession to the experience.

During the early 1970s my involvement in the teaching of American women's history began to change my casual approach to media of popular culture. Conversations with students alerted me to the importance of contemporary television images of women—initially as derogatory and exploitive examples of anti-feminism—but progressively as a source that contained valuable evidence of current public attitudes toward women. Daytime soap operas and commercials dwelt on the perceived concerns of housewives—child-rearing, marriage relationships, infidelity, divorce, consumerism—while prime time fictional programs revealed some awareness of single and married females in the marketplace, women who defined themselves as feminists, and politically active housewives. Although television offered few role models to the enlightened feminist community, the dominant means of mass communication in the American society of the 1970s seemed to mirror the range of "possible female characterizations" that an audience of millions found acceptable.[1]

This assumption was palatable for two reasons. First, national ratings determined the life or death of programs based on fictionalized scripts. Any dramatic series or situation comedy or soap opera that presented characterizations or themes far in advance (or far behind) general standards of public approval did not survive the Nielson or Arbutron tests. Both the major networks and local television stations deleted, continued, or substituted programs in mid-season depending on how the audience at home voted in ratings surveys. Second, as the modern women's movement generated a public dialogue on women's issues, the images of women on television began to change, suggesting that media of popular culture responded—at times swiftly—to changes in public attitudes.[2]

This analysis is not new. In her now famous book, *The Feminine Mystique,* Betty Friedan noted the rather abrupt change in the nature of heroines in short stories published in women's magazines in the late 1940s. The image of the "New Woman"—a female who passionately searched for an individual identity—had predominated in the 1930s and through the World War II years, Friedan wrote. By 1949, however, "Fulfillment as a woman had only one definition for American women—the housewife-mother."[3]

Friedan observed this pattern in television programs of the entire post-war period. From its inception as a medium of popular culture, television had embraced and reflected the image of women as "strangely helpless, passive, not very bright" housewives. Dependent upon massive public acceptance for its economic survival, television apparently mirrored what the audience found comfortable. Through the 1950s and into the 1960s, the "dreary, dumb wife" met approval in the same manner as the Stepanfetchit blackface had in an earlier era.[4]

The recent women's movement, Friedan suggested in the 1970s, had greatly altered Americans' attitudes toward women and the television programs of the decade were indicative of those changes. Evening programs now presented women who were "bright, attractive, sexy, and gutsy," heroines who acted "adventurously in their own lives." The popularity of situation comedies such as "The Mary Tyler Moore Show," "Maude," "Rhoda," "One Day at a Time," or dramatic productions like "Police Woman" showed the extent to which the public was willing to consider "the various realities" of women's lives.[5]

In her article, Friedan linked the changing images of women on television directly to "the formal actions of the women's movement." Speaking before a seminar of the West Coast Association of Women Historians in the spring of 1978, Columbia Television Pictures' producer Robert Sweeney qualified Friedan's reasoning. While networks were sensitive to pressure groups, he explained, their "ultimate patrons" were the millions of viewers who voted for programs by their channel selections. In the long run, Sweeney noted, "we reflect what the audience finds comfortable." The emergence of independent, forceful heroines in television programs in the 1970s reflected the *public's* acceptance of this type of woman, Sweeney implied. While the women's movement was unquestionably important, its major impact was not as a pressure group working on network personnel, but as a movement which encouraged Americans to reevaluate their views of women. In Sweeney's view, the new feminine images on television reflected the public's comfort with a more diverse presentation of women's capacities and situations. In other words, network television did not lead public taste—it followed the demands of the audience.[6]

Since the major networks have recently faced law suits which attempt to define their accountability, Sweeney's suggestion that television reflects existing public perceptions more than it influences its audience's views may be approached fairly with skepticism. The extent to which television affects viewers' behavior remains an important and unanswered question, one which continues to deserve the attention of scholars in the behavioral sciences.

On the other hand, the perspective suggested by Columbia producer Sweeney is attractive to the historian. If the most popular medium of mass entertainment in our time *reflects* extant public attitudes on a variety of topics—including the acceptable roles and behaviors of women—then perhaps motion picture feature films produced in the first half of the twentieth century also offer significant evidence of earlier public perceptions on "woman's place."

Before the "small screen" became the most popular medium of visual entertainment in the United States, films occupied a similar place in American life. The opulent movie palaces built during the prosperous twenties remained full of customers in the years of the Great Depression and movie attendance soared to record-breaking proportions during the Second World War. Whatever the state of the economy or political affairs or personal pocketbooks, "Americans needed their movies," wrote Andrew Bergman. "[They] had come to play too important a role in their lives to be considered just another luxury item." Current statistics show that Americans are equally attached to their television sets. While only 81 percent of households of white families have refrigerators, 96 percent possess a television set; for black households, the percentages are, respectively, 73 and 93.[7]

Until recently, intellectuals and pressure groups who interested themselves in the visual media limited their concern to the influence (good or bad) that movies or television exerted on a passive group of viewers. The literature on this topic reaches back to the early decades of the twentieth century when movies were short flickering images played on nickel machines in store-front shacks, and the continuing presence of this school is apparent in the written and verbal announcements preceding television programs thought to contain sensitive material.[8]

While the dialogue centering on the influence of visual media is unquestionably valuable, historians have started to consider motion pictures in a different light. Noting the manner in which television programs of the past decade mirrored changing public attitudes toward women, blacks, Mexican-Americans, Puerto Ricans, soldiers, young people—even homosexuals and prostitutes—scholars began to consider the possibility that movies were also reflectors and preservers of the public attitudes of their time. The impetus for this new look at film came from several sources: the emergence of scholars who belonged to "the film generation;" a new interest in popular culture as media equipment became more readily accessible to lecturers; and, most importantly perhaps, the stretching of the definition of social history. As academics and professional writers turned their attention to recapturing the pasts of anonymous or non-literate peoples, traditional written sources seemed inadequate. Historians concerned with understanding the experiences and culture of black Americans led the way in the search for different forms of historical evidence, but scholars of American women's history followed closely behind. And, among the often obscure, long neglected sources that received attention from those interested in the past of American women were Hollywood motion picture feature films.[9]

As my interest in American women's history grew, I was presented with a happy conjuncture of scholarly writing. Provocative articles which explored the methodological questions surrounding the use of film as historical evidence were appearing at the same time that pioneers in American women's history were emphasizing the need to explore sources that might offer new insights into the past experiences of American women. Moreover, movies seemed to conform to the same theories applied to television. The ratings that guided the decisions of Hollywood producers were the clinks of money at the box-office—one best-selling feature film inevitably created a series of duplicates. And when critics accused the film industry of pandering to crude tastes, Hollywood's ready answer was "we give our viewers what they want."[10]

Professional writers interested in the images of women in feature films expressed annoyance and dissatisfaction with the complacency implied in the standard Hollywood response. The two most comprehensive works exploring the film industry's characterizations of women through its history, Marjorie Rosen's *Popcorn Venus: Women, Movies and the American Dream* (New York, 1973) and Molly Haskell's *From Reverence to Rape: The Treatment of Women in the Movies* (New York, 1973) were frankly hostile to Hollywood's productions. Pointing to the male dominance of movie studios, both authors concluded that films mainly offered demeaning and limiting stereotypes of women.

While conceding that "an image . . . is molded from prevailing audience attitudes," Marjorie Rosen insisted that the American public itself held a deeply erroneous view of women—one that the film industry tragically encouraged. The glamor and intensity of the cinema magnified the artificiality of this "Popcorn Venus," entrancing viewers, but also revealing that the image of any woman on the screen was "a delectable but insubstantial hybrid of cultural distortions." Similarly, Molly Haskell chastised the movie industry for its role in perpetuating "The Big Lie" of women's inferiority. This myth, she explained, "[is] so deeply ingrained in our social behavior that merely to recognize it is to risk unraveling the entire fabric of civilization."

Both Rosen's and Haskell's works were ambitious attempts to survey Hollywood's treatment of women throughout the twentieth century. While each contains its especial "intriguing potpourri of information," the books are basically flawed and superficial (Haskell's work contains neither footnotes nor a bibliography). No comprehensible sample of movies is delineated by either author; they plunge glibly into decades ("The Twenties," "The Thirties") or categories ("Emerging From Victorianism," "The Woman's Film"), apparently deciding which films to discuss by choosing from their own private repertoires. Haskell finds some of the major stars of the 1940s praiseworthy (Jean Arthur, Barbara Stanwyck, Katherine Hepburn, Bette Davis), noting that they projected "images of strong, vibrant women sparring quite expertly with their men"—even if they capitulated in marriage at the movie's end. Rosen also finds heroines of merit in the forties' movies, commenting that "female strength" replaced the "bitchery" and "frivolity" usually associated with women, particularly in films produced during the World War II years.

Haskell's and Rosen's critiques were written in the early 1970s, a period in American society when feminists were pressing for recognition and a broader public dialogue on women's issues. Both books were influenced by this milieu, although *Popcorn Venus* is the more obviously reactive. "Again and again," reviewer Stephen Farber observed, "Rosen scores early films for failing to express a contemporary feminist point of view."[11] Molly Haskell tried to avoid this problem, identifying herself as "a film critic first and a feminist second." Yet the historical scope of her work and the multitudinous films included in her study demanded some type of framework beyond aesthetic appeal, and Haskell eventually tied her piquant but awkward work together by coming to the same conclusions as Rosen: In the heyday of their influence, American movies had, with few exceptions, presented unattractive, confining images of women to the American public. Rather than leading popular taste toward more realistic conceptions of women's talents, Hollywood had succumbed to the mythology of the time, striving as energetically as other American institutions to keep women in their place.

Although Rosen's and Haskell's books provide entertaining reading and occasional moments of serious analysis, their interpretation of the images of women in films appears simplistic and incomplete. A mutual devotion to a limited definition of feminism permeates their works, curtailing the reader's imagination and obscuring the complexity of the film medium. While both books attempt an historical survey, the authors commit the too common error of imposing present values on past eras.

Motion picture feature films are approached more fruitfully as documents of their own time, documents which can illuminate Americans' perceptions of women's roles in the past. As early as 1969, historian Gerda Lerner suggested a different approach to women's history, calling for a conceptual framework that went beyond the belief that "the history of woman is important only as representing the history of an oppressed group and its struggle against its oppressors." Lerner proposed several new directions for scholars concerned with the history of American women. Among them was one especially appropriate to researchers interested in media of popular culture such as feature motion pictures. "It would be most worthwhile," Professor Lerner wrote, "to distinguish the ideas held at any given moment in regard to woman's proper place from what was actually woman's status at that time." Since there seemed to be a considerable gap between popular perceptions and the realities of women's lives, social historians needed to examine the prevailing folklore of specific periods with some care, determining the importance "of ideas about women in the general ordering of society."[12]

In an article in *Societas,* Eugene C. McCreary offered a theoretical basis for the use of film in such a study. The historian interested in assessing public attitudes in past decades of the twentieth century would find the feature movie document a rich source, he wrote. The financial dependency of the Hollywood industry upon movie-goers inevitably made it "more than usually sensitive to mass interests and mass desires." Movies, therefore, offered the scholar evidence "of the elusive and unstated, of social mores, attitudes and values," as well as a rare picture "of the psycho-social realities of specific societies at given periods of time."[13]

Other academics joined McCreary in championing motion pictures as research evidence. In a thought-provoking article, Michael Isenberg pointed out that "historians [had] long valued the aesthetic approach to the study of culture." Identifying themselves with the intellectual community, historians had disdained cultural artifacts created for profit and mass audiences. The desire to associate with the taste and beauty of aesthetic works of art or the high thought in books written by people of their own kind had led historians to an elitist concept of culture, Isenberg maintained. In his view, American intellectual histories were primarily records of the private culture of the nation. Evidence which spoke of popular ideas or popular culture was ignored because it seemed beneath historical attention. According to this somewhat angry champion of fresh sources, products of America's machine culture were especially disliked, for the commercial cinema seemed to pander "shamelessly to emotion and crude taste." Isenberg sharply demanded a different approach to film evidence, urging historians to recognize their biases and to consider movies as they would other types of evidence of the past. "Using only aesthetic judgment is to denigrate those qualities which make history a viable profession," Isenberg proclaimed.[14]

The writings of scholars such as Lerner, McCreary, Isenberg, and others conveyed a persuasive argument for a historical study of the images of women in motion picture feature films. Since Rosen's and Haskell's books had disclosed the monumental problems involved in canvassing the twentieth century, I determined to select a specific and limited time frame for my study, an approach that Andrew Bergman had taken with convincing success in his *We're In The Money: Depression America And Its Films* (New York, 1971). It also seemed important to delineate a sample of movies with some care. The film industry was amazingly prolific during its reign as America's chief form of mass entertainment; despite the scarcity of materials during World War II, Hollywood produced more than 500 movies each year. Without definitive guidelines to discipline our study of the evidence at hand, films could be used to prove any point of view.

My decision to concentrate on the top-grossing war films produced during the years of the United States' involvement in World War II was influenced by several factors. First, the war years were described as vital ones for American women by historians interested in the process of social change. Noting that the war had generated new enthusiasm for female workers as well as lucrative jobs in the marketplace for them, scholars such as William Chafe suggested that World War II had encouraged American women's bid for equality by providing females with genuine economic options. In the historical literature, the only events of similar magnitude for women in the twentieth century were the First and Second Women's Movements. Movies and popular novels of the 1910s and 1920s, and television in the 1970s, showed that "the normative definition of 'woman's place' set forth by the dominant culture" was altered by both women's movements.[15] Would the movies of the war years reflect a similarly pressured redefinition of woman's place, one that coincided with scholars' descriptions of the new social realities of women's lives? The answer seemed most likely to be found in the best-selling war movies (the films of greatest propaganda content) produced in the years, 1941-1945.

If these films contained images of women who were committed to careers or jobs in the marketplace, then the war could be credited with encouraging an expanded view of female capability. Conversely, if the women characters in top-grossing movies designed to evoke patriotism remained devoted to women's traditional roles (sweetheart, wife, and mother), then World War II might be seen more properly as an event that widened the gap between the public's perceptions of women's roles and the actual lifestyles and activities of American females. If the latter were the case, an argument could be made for the war's retardative effect on women's quest for equality in American society. Rather than strengthening the public's view of women as independent and autonomous persons, the war might have encouraged Americans to link democracy and freedom with women's traditional positions in society, thus committing society to a defense of these roles in the post-war years.

The second factor that drew me to the World War II period was my discovery of a government agency that monitored Hollywood productions from early 1942 through the summer of 1943. The Bureau of Motion Pictures (Domestic Branch) was an agency within the bureaucracy of the Office of War Information, the organization charged with explaining the war to Americans. Analysts employed by the BMP read Hollywood producers' scripts, watched preview versions of films, developed their own guidelines as to what constituted an acceptable movie for domestic consumption, and left valuable records of their attempts to sway motion picture producers and directors from what BMP personnel considered limiting or demeaning portrayals of Americans. The liberals in the Bureau of Motion Pictures expressed dissatisfaction with select movies' depiction of the internal enemy, black Americans, Japanese Americans, and American women. In fact, analysts of the short-lived agency worked with some diligence to improve Hollywood's depiction of women in war films, but their labors apparently met box-office approval in only one instance. Although the ill-kept records of the Bureau prohibit definitive statements, written evidence links the BMP's efforts solely to the top-grossing movie, *So Proudly We Hail.*[16]

The third factor that led me to the period, 1941–1945, was the availability of box-office figures (from three sources) that allowed a reasonable determination of the top-grossing feature movies of those years. If people voted from their pocketbooks to have a satisfying experience, as Audience Research Studies conducted in the 1940s indicated, then the best-sellers of any year provided the best mirror of public perceptions toward women's roles.[17]

Finally, by limiting my film sample to include only the most popular war movies produced during the years 1941–1945, it became possible to examine individual films in depth.[18] This format, I felt, provided new room to explore both the characteristics of the heroines that the public found acceptable, and the importance that Americans attached, in popular thought, to what might be called "women's culture," a term I use to describe the institutions and activities—marriage, home, family-connections, child-rearing, spiritual life, care for the dead, church involvement—to which women devoted much of their time and energy in the era to be examined.

Acknowledgments

This study would not have materialized without the encouragement offered by many people. Although the final responsibility rests with me, I wish to thank those who have helped me shape my thinking and writing.

I am grateful to Professor Otis L. Graham, Jr., who complimented my study by giving it his serious, prompt attention during several stages of its evolution. In addition, the criticisms and suggestions of Professor Patricia Cohen and Professor Francis Dutra were immensely helpful to me in completing the final manuscript. I wish to thank both for their careful, thoughtful readings. I am further indebted to several persons at UMI Research Press, most particularly Professor Robert Berkhofer, series editor, and Christine Hammes, my cheerful and able production editor.

This manuscript was also made possible by the Woodrow Wilson Foundation. I very much appreciated the Fellowship grant in Women's Studies which allowed me the opportunity to travel and complete my research.

The staff of the Motion Picture Division of the Library of Congress, Washington, D.C., was amazingly efficient and gracious during my months in their presence. Their receptivity to my needs aided me greatly in the early phases of my research as did the interest of the staff of the Audio-visual Division of the National Archives and that of the librarians of the Washington National Records Center in Suitland, Maryland. The curators of the Film Archives at the University of California, Los Angeles, and the personnel of Learning Resources at the University of California, Santa Barbara, were equally valuable. My research would have consumed a much longer period without the information supplied by these knowledgeable professionals.

I also wish to thank the circle of women and men, whether colleagues, students, family, or friends, who willingly listened and offered their comments as I struggled with the ideas my research presented. My lengthy discussions with Lyn Goldfarb, Joan Beatty, Barbara Russell,

Rolfe Buzzell, Lillian Webb, Miriam Pearson, Perry Kaufman, and John Mraz were especially helpful in solidifying my thoughts.

My parents have always been among my most valuable assets, as have my sisters, my brothers-in-law, and their families. The in-law family I gained in recent years, Bob, Nina, and David Bishop, has also added richness to my life. It is a pleasure to thank all of these people for the sustenance so freely given.

Finally, I dedicate this book to the person who has been truly indispensable to me in these months of research and writing, Ron Bishop, my spouse. More than any other person, he made this work possible through his generous support and constant encouragement.

                                                        M. Joyce Baker
                                                Summerland, California
                                                        October 1980

Introduction

Backing Up the Front Lines . . . Women at War

The lifestyles of American women were jolted considerably during World War II. As the United States geared itself for unconditional victory over the Axis powers, official government policy urged Americans to stretch their visions of women's capabilities, and this message was swiftly echoed in the popular media. In this barrage of advice, women were asked to conduct their traditional homemaking tasks with greater efficiency and compassion while simultaneously they were spurred to take jobs outside the home—in war industries or the military. A familiar government slogan ran, "The more women at war—the sooner we'll win."[1]

In the first year of the war, after alluding to women's obligations to servicemen, Eleanor Roosevelt suggested that "wives, sisters, or mothers of the Army fighting on the production front have a very great responsibility." Since the war might well be won or lost in production quotas, Mrs. Roosevelt encouraged women to see that man-hours of work were not forfeited due to illnesses, accidents, or strikes. Toward this end, the homemaker's most important objective was to keep her family well, both physically and emotionally. Thus mothers and wives must use their executive ability to see that the family ingest proper food and get sufficient sleep. That requires, Mrs. Roosevelt wrote, "persuading them to do what is good for them in spite of their frequent desire to ignore it." Responsible homemakers were also budget-conscious, saving 10 percent of the family's income for savings stamps and bonds, and collecting scrap metal, rubber and tin cans. "The biggest and most difficult responsibility, however," Mrs. Roosevelt insisted, "has to do with her [the homemaker's] attitude toward life." Women's discomforts, whether they be based in worries about sons, husbands, and brothers abroad or restrictions at home, must be smothered, for no man with an unhappy atmosphere in his home could produce to his maximum. "His spirit is dependent on her spirit," Mrs. Roosevelt continued. "Let us remember that our smile in the morning may mean that extra bullet which saved some mother's son from death."[2]

At the same time women were counseled to be receptive and competent in their traditional domains, government bulletins solicited their participation in the marketplace and the armed forces, and the popular media quickly picked up the refrain. National Defense posters showed women workers in kerchiefs and slacks, proclaiming them "Soldiers Without Guns," while WAVES recruiting material insisted "It's a Women's War Too!" Rosie the Riveter became a popular heroine (particularly after the *Saturday Evening Post* cover of 1943) and magazines provided personal accounts of women in transition in articles such as *Harper's* "From Housewife to Shipfitter."[3]

Radio broadcasts carried a diversity of messages, emphasizing womanpower as "a limitless, ever-flowing source of moral and physical energy—working—for victory." Spot announcements written by the Office of War Information's Radio Bureau staff reminded Americans that "our soldiers [*sic*] don't care if the hands who made his gun are male or female, old or young, immigrant or native stock," while radio dramatizations featured women workers as courageous patriots performing essential duties.[4]

Newsreels devoted special attention to women in the armed forces, showing WACS and WAVES adjusting to military routine and "relieving thousands of men for duty at the front" by assuming a variety of jobs—typists, chauffeurs, air tower control operators, cooks, and telephone operators. A year into the war, Paramount News carried a special "Meet the WAFS" film clip, illustrating members of the Women's Auxiliary Ferrying Squadron handling piloting duties with ease, while WACS filmed on training maneuvers in jeeps and trucks were dubbed "Rough Riders" by the narrator. News releases also reported on women's new roles in industry, commenting on the "girls' quick proficiency" with intricate machinery in Navy yards and war factories. The special needs of female employees were accented in news briefs outlining the goals of the WOWs (Women Ordnance Workers) whose organization was designed to promote healthful working conditions and friendship among female war plant workers. Similarly, footage on child nurseries explained their value in freeing mothers' minds to work. Children were shown eating nutritious food, receiving health care and learning through their interactions with one another "how to live in a strange, new, ever-changing world."[5]

Popular movies also joined the chorus of voices and images enticing women to greater efforts both at home and in traditional male domains. *Since You Went Away* (1944), David O. Selznick's ode to the home front, focused on a wife and mother who graciously managed her head-of-household responsibilities and a war job. The heroic stature of nurses was dramatized in *So Proudly We Hail* (1943) while *Here Come the Waves* (1945) offered an inside view of women's life in the military. Alternatives for wives of servicemen were posited in *Thirty Seconds Over Tokyo* (1944) and *Winged Victory* (1944). And further films of persuasion, often the most effective ones, dwelt on the lives of women subjected to total war, women either under fascist control or threatened with imminent take-over. The image of Mrs. Miniver (in the movie of the same name), comforting her family in an insecure bomb shelter, became a part of the public consciousness, defining war for many women. Other heroines were equally important—stoic Ilsa in *Casablanca,* the young, determined Nazi-fighter in *Hitler's Children,* and the cruelly betrayed Tama in *Behind the Rising Sun.*[6]

The net result of the clamorous attention paid to the reserve labor force of American women was a drastic change in their activities. As jobs opened in the wartime marketplace, women responded to the patriotic flourishes of government posters, radio broadcasts, magazine articles and film footage by attempting to keep both the home fires and the furnaces of production burning. The female labor force increased by 6.5 million or 57 percent during the war years, boosting the number of women workers to nearly 20 million by 1945. And, significantly, the profile of the woman worker also changed. She was no longer single, but married; no longer under 35, but over 35. The wives of America were working outside the home, often pulling up family roots in order to do so (7 million women moved from their county of residence during the war, a startling increase from pre-war times), and in the process, women were forced to balance the needs of their families and the demands of a breadwinner's role. "In the eyes of many observers," William Chafe wrote, "women's experience during the war years amounted to a revolution."[7]

The revolution appeared to take place in public attitudes as much as women's activities. Early in the war bureaucrats in the federal government had isolated the major resistances to the fullest use of women in "community traditions" and "employer prejudices." Intelligence-gatherer Eugene Katz suggested that "The German slogan: Kindler [*sic*], Juche [*sic*], Kirche (children, kitchen, church), while anathema to the 'modern woman' does strike a responsive chord in the conservative tradition of most American communities." Acting from this framework, Katz wrote, "Employers implement their general attitudes of masculine superiority with rationalizations about women's inability to perform the required work." By 1944, the government-inspired campaign to extend Americans' views of women's capabilities appeared to have changed public attitudes in major ways. Male employers now accepted female laborers with alacrity, often praising them in uncompromising terms. Bomber-producer Glenn L. Martin insisted, "There will always be a place for the skilled woman worker in the aircraft industry. Many jobs she performs as well as men, and some she performs better." And Eleanor Roosevelt spoke to the issue of "children, kitchen, church" in a 1944 article. Some women, she suggested, were not talented with children and actually resented the work of a home. In these instances, the solution was to "find someone to do that job who loves it, and release the mother to a different kind of work." Moreover, the sheer numbers of women who, by 1944, had ably performed dual home and marketplace roles appeared to discredit the conservative stance that had been so worrisome earlier to federal officials.[8]

But, as is often the case, patriotic statements and actions in time of war reflect only one kind of reality. The drastic changes in women's life-styles during World War II had not been accompanied by a lengthy public debate, the kind of social quarrel that had, for example, kept the "woman question" alive to Americans a decade before World War I and the suffrage victory of 1920. World war—a temporary crisis—had provided the impetus for change in women's usual roles, and the allegiance to traditional sexual divisions smoldered quietly beneath the patriotic veneer.[9]

The most obvious indication of the limited public discussion was the government program itself. Women were urged to address their responsibilities at home more seriously because of war priorities—and they were asked to consider jobs outside the home for the same reason. "This is a Tough War," federal bulletins proclaimed; "Women of America . . . step forth and find your place in the war."[10]

The dictum to step forth was urged upon women with little consideration for its potential implications. War was an aberration, a time in which all citizens performed unique feats, and women's efforts—particularly in the marketplace—were depicted in just this manner. The attempt of federal policymakers to create superwomen was no different from their effort to make supermen soldiers from raw civilian materials. Sacrifice was the key word for all Americans, and under these circumstances, it is not surprising that government officials did not encourage a heated dialogue on the suitability of traditional sexual roles. While child care centers, equal pay, promotional opportunities, easy access to markets, and reasonable living conditions would have aided women workers enormously, few policymakers were willing to encourage the kind of controversy that would have accompanied legislation that bolstered far-reaching changes in the existing patterns of family life and male-female relationships.[11]

The popular media echoed the government's objectives, intensifying the need for sacrifice, and ignoring the genuine problems that arose in that effort. Even in war the lines of traditional sexual demarcation held. Radio, magazines, newspapers, and films were filled with patriotic enthusiasm for women's war efforts, but they also revealed a strong attachment to conventional ideas of woman's place. The same newsreels that lauded WACS' and WAVES' accomplishments also sent forth ambivalent messages; women were referred to as "regular soldiers," but their femininity was stressed by news commentators. A United News release on WACS' arrival in England in 1943 explained that "their first desire . . . like all women's [was] to make themselves at home," and a Paramount News report rhapsodized on the womanly look of the "snappy rigs of the gals who will rule the waves," suggesting the women's continued interest in "female concerns" such as clothes styles and an attractive appearance.[12]

Popular movies about the war reflected the same ambiguity. Heroines were often ambitious and capable war fighters, but they were, nevertheless, women. As members of a distinctive breed of social animal, women (like men) had unique characteristics, thoughts, and behaviors, which, films implied, best suited them for particular functions in society. War upset the natural balance, separating men and women and forcing good persons of either sex to extraordinary measures. Men left their country to fight in the Pacific or Europe or Africa in defense of the American home, and women left their homes to provide the war machinery for soldiers abroad. "Mom" and "apple pie" were familiar symbols of freedom in movie dialogue, and women's entry into the war-time labor force undoubtedly raised worrisome questions among soldiers—would the American home be destroyed in their effort to save it? Films offered a reassuring answer; for the most part, women were as eager as men to maintain the old ways.[13]

It is not surprising to find popular movies firmly enmeshed in the traditional lore that had frustrated feminists throughout the twentieth century. F. Scott Fitzgerald's last tycoon, a tough-minded film producer, described the parameters of movie-making succinctly in the author's final novel: "Our condition is that we have to take people's own favorite folklore and dress it up and give it back to them." Yet it is also this aspect of film that gives it a dynamic value in deciphering Americans' attitudes toward women during the war years. What were the old ways associated with women that Americans prized in the early 1940s? Did sexual roles blur if women worked outside the home? Two very different films, Frank Capra's *Meet John Doe* and Howard Hawks' *Sergeant York*, "Hollywood's first solid contribution to national defense," offer some clues.[14]

Perceptions of Women on the Eve of War

Sergeant York (Warner Brothers, 1941)

Released during the summer of 1941, Warner Brothers' *Sergeant York* became the major box-office attraction of that year, earning double the theater gross of the average movie. The film dramatized the life of Alvin York, a well known hero of the Great War of 1917–1918, who thereafter became permanently confused in the public mind with lanky and boyish Gary Cooper. York himself emerged from a jealously guarded private existence to attend the July 31st premiere, leading presidential assistant Lowell Mellett to suggest that "The fellow is sincerely lending himself to the purposes of defense." Mellett felt the event merited President Roosevelt's attention and he urged Stephen Early to include a meeting with York on F.D.R.'s agenda. " 'Sergeant York,' " Mellett wrote, "is about the finest thing thus far on the screen for the promotion of national morale. It is the sort of thing that we'd like everybody to see."[1]

Although the movie was set in an earlier historical period, the story of America's most celebrated hero of World War I was obviously relevant to audiences facing issues of national defense and war preparedness. Lewis Jacobs observed, "The film subtly and astutely rallied popular feeling for participation in the war. [It was] an eloquent advocate for persuading pacifist-minded men to become war recruits."[2]

Sergeant York may have tipped the scales toward enlistment for many young male viewers of the early war years. Certainly Alvin York's story provided draft-age men with a model to emulate. But the impact of *Sergeant York* was not limited to questions of pacifism or soldiering. A closer study of the film reveals a stirring description of the traditional American success legend. The movie was a family film, designed to entertain audiences while verifying important American values such as the possibility of upward mobility, the significance of family and religion in one's personal development, the binding ties of romantic love, and the necessity of protecting, in time of crisis, democracy and freedom as represented by the United States.

Through the York clan (Mother York, Alvin, and his two siblings) the film dramatized the components of family life in an impoverished agrarian society that enabled an uneducated, backwoods farm boy to become a national hero. And, in this process, the influence of York's mother and the girl he wished to marry are seen as second only to that of God.[3]

In this sense, *Sergeant York* spoke to the female half of the movie audience. Since motion picture producers (even the Warner Brothers, so noted for social consciousness) were not yet appealing to women to join the war effort actively, *Sergeant York* captured the old ways in which women were valued in the public consciousness. A careful reading of the film suggests that women's culture was different from men's, but important, nonetheless.[4]

Sergeant York, directed by Howard Hawks, opens on a sober, patriotic note. Although the film will explore one man's heroism in combat, the words of dedication following the movie credits reflect Americans' antipathy toward war. The inscription on the screen urges viewers to have "faith . . . that a day will come when man will live in peace" and the propriety of this wish is underscored by the plaintive strains of "America."[5]

York's film odyssey begins during the pre-World War I years in the remote mountains of Tennessee among hard-working, God-fearing, "hell-raisin'" folk. In the opening scene, York falls in the last category. The camera focuses on a plain, woodsy church filled with simple people lifting their voices to God in a rousing hymn reminiscent of the Mormon Tabernacle Choir. As the country preacher (Walter Brennan) starts his sermon, the worshipful scene is interrupted by the sound of shots and boisterous, drunken yells. To the delight of his drinking partners, sharpshooter Alvin York is practicing his art by grooving his initials in the trunk of a churchyard tree. Pastor Rosier Pile and his congregation react with angry mutterings, but there is no wholesale condemnation of York, for Mother York (Margaret Wycherly) is within the church, among them, and her worn face reflects chagrin and suffering at her son's antics.

As the sound of retreating hoofbeats is heard, the camera lingers on Mrs. York, introducing the audience to one of the persons of greatest influence in Alvin York's life. A spunky and compassionate woman who commands the respect of her close-knit community, the widowed Mother York (for so she is called throughout the film) is a large, buxom woman whose face mirrors endurance and fortitude. She moves through the movie with determined, stoical movements, accepting her lonely role as family matriarch, even as it saps her life resources. Relying upon her three children, especially the oldest, Alvin, for the toil that generates their livelihood from the stubborn Tennessee soil, she maintains her control of the family by alternate doses of love and punishment. When, at her summons, Alvin returns home from his spree, she greets him at the cabin door with a bucket of water which she calmly throws in his face—then just as matter-of-factly, she invites him to sit down for his favorite breakfast, which she has just finished preparing.

In troubled or happy times, religion is Mother York's mainstay; her belief in a fundamentalist God and her involvement in her church provide the spiritual resources that allow her to persevere, and it is not surprising that she sees faith as the salvation for Alvin. Interpreting his rambunctiousness as the devilry of a man without a purpose, she worries over Alvin and finally asks for outside help. Conceding to Pastor Pile that Alvin is slipping out of her control, she pleads with him to warn her son of the pitfalls of the devil's influence, but she also asks the pastor to understand Alvin's plight: "It's hard work growing corn out of rocks."

The preacher speaks to Alvin, but the boy is as deaf to Pastor Pile's words as to his mother's attempts to convert him. In the first section of the film, inspiration and purpose will come to Alvin from a more secular source—he falls in love.

The importance of Alvin's discovery of love is portrayed in Hollywood's grand romantic style. Our first glimpse of Gracie Williams (Joan Leslie) shows her in a demure, girlish pose, curled up in a rocking chair on the front porch of her family's rustic home, subtly preening herself while combing her long, dark hair. York rushes by, involved with his brother on a hunting chase, then abruptly halts as he becomes aware of the vision of loveliness before him. As a romantic theme swells in the background, York remains rooted, struck with love as he will later be struck with lightning on his road to religious conversion. Gracie's response to York's rapt admiration is feminine coyness. She scowls and turns away, although the camera follows her, allowing us to see her immense secret enjoyment at the impact her prettiness has made.

Winning the hand of the petite Gracie now becomes York's consuming goal. Although the audience is never in doubt (we know they are destined for one another), York must struggle to overcome his past reputation of shiftlessness. Gracie sets the standards for marriageability in this important game of love, and she enforces her conviction that "hell-raisin" characteristics are not proper qualities in a husband by dangling rivals in Alvin's face. Moreover, Gracie belongs to the upper crust of Tennessee mountain society, those farmers whose land has retained fertility, and Alvin must prove himself a capable breadwinner before she will take his affection seriously.

Inspired by love, Alvin York sets forth on the path of upward mobility: he determines to buy a parcel of the rich bottomland in the region of the Williams' farm. Mother York is fearful when she learns the reason for her son's exuberant singing and new devotion to a steady life. "Folks on the bottomland look down on folks on top," she warns Alvin. "Ain't no changing it." Her husband practically killed himself trying to get bottomland, she explains; the soil in their possession is all the York family has had for generations, and the wisdom of the past would teach them to be content. The family history has not eroded Mother York's belief in the American Dream entirely, however, and when York insists, "I'm a gonna get it," she replies with a quiet smile, "Maybe you will."

The next portion of *Sergeant York* is dominated by Alvin's efforts to obtain bottomland. He drives himself, undertaking any kind of work which pays wages, ripping out stumps, moving rocks, exerting himself both day and night. Both his mother and "Miss Gracie" share his agony and lend encouragement. His mother awakens during the nights to pull the covers over an exhausted Alvin, lingering over his spent body to pray for his success, while Gracie appears at twilight while Alvin is plowing a field to inspire him with her love. This latter moment is the romantic highlight in the film, revealing Hollywood's perception of how two people behave when they have been tangled in love's mysterious web. York is plodding along behind an ancient plow, dressed in overalls, a sweatstained shirt, and a floppy hat which has protected his head from the scorching sun during his long day's work. Gracie appears, dressed modestly in a long print dress with a crocheted shawl thrown around her head. She has come to tell Alvin something, but he must divine what it is, for her discomfort and stuttering reveals that she can only express her feelings with her eyes and manner—words are too difficult and threatening. The physical overtures must come from York; Gracie can only invite them with an alluring, coquettish presence and an adoring gaze. As the rays of the setting sun establish a brilliant background, the romantic theme amplifies to a crescendo as York finally grabs Gracie and embraces her. Although Gracie flees quickly after this moment of screen intimacy, her mission has been accomplished, and the two are pledged on an affective level, regardless of the barriers that may occur in the future.

The obstacles come swiftly as the film concentrates solely on Alvin York and the events which will catapult him to fame as a war hero. Betrayed by the man who promised to sell him bottomland, York returns to his whiskey haunts and his reckless lifestyle. Drunk and embittered, he sets out one rain-tossed night to kill Tompkins, the traitor who destroyed his dream. Lightning strikes near him and when he recovers consciousness, he discovers his rifle has been reduced to a smoldering hunk of metal. Providentially close to the woodsy meeting house, York stumbles toward the voices singing, "In the Sweet Bye and Bye," convinced at last that God exists and has personally taken time to influence his life. As his ecstatic mother beams and Gracie smiles through her tears, Pastor Pile baptizes Alvin while the congregation joyfully stamps out "Give Me That Old Time Religion."

York's conversion to religion, his acceptance of the civilized mode of life urged by his mother and sweetheart, now pose the moral dilemma which made the film popular fare for audiences in 1941. Devoted to a literal interpretation of the Bible, York refuses to join in the enthusiasm for war when the United States enters World War I in 1917. "War is agin the Book," he declares and continues planning his life with Gracie. However, despite the help of Pastor Pile and several appeals, York's application for a conscientious objector status is rejected and he eventually must go into the army, for as the preacher says, "It's the law." His leavetaking from his family is strained and awkward, full of suppressed feelings and silent, meaningful looks. The film implies that the Yorks are simple people who have exhausted their alternatives and must now accept their fate. As Alvin rides away, his mother and sister stand stoically by their wooden fence (Gracie has already escaped to the hills to mourn in private) and when her daughter asks, "Ma, what are they a fightin' for?" Mother York can only reply in anguish, "I don't rightly know, child, I don't rightly know."

Alvin York now enters the thoroughly male-dominated world of the U. S. Army. Quiet, cooperative and enormously skillful with a rifle, he makes friends and broadens his knowledge (learning what a subway is from a New Yorker) but is regarded with suspicion by his sergeant and some militant officers because of his history of conscientious objection. York is not to be bereft of the kind of support and understanding he received from his mother and girlfriend, however. The values of compassion and caring are represented in this film segment by high army officers, who, unlike York's sergeant, listen to and endorse York's feelings about killing. There is no question, his major explains, of the importance of the Bible's admonitions, but how are democracy and freedom to be preserved if one does not fight? Pleading with York to take a furlough and think about it, the major hands him a book which he insists York must weigh in conjunction with the Bible—a history of the United States.

In this most important decision in the film, York is existentially alone. There is no heated family discussion, for both Mother York and Gracie accept that Alvin must confront his conscience and determine his own actions. Whatever hardships the women must endure as a result of York's decision are secondary in importance to Alvin's spiritual needs.

Therefore, York sits alone on a Tennessee mountaintop, his books and his dog his only companions. Once again he receives a message; the wind flips the pages of his Bible to the strategic phrase: "Render unto Caesar that which is Caesar's and unto God that which is God's." Satisfied, York leaves his peaceful homeland, and the film plunges the viewers into the European War.

Women exist only in the minds of men in the trenches in France and exploding shells and immense fatigue do not create an environment for dwelling on warm memories. The raw American troops, Sergeant York among them, are initiated to the grim reality of instant death or survival that depends on physical prowess and luck. "If one's got your name on it, there's nothing you can do," a grimy Englishman says laconically.

Sergeant York becomes a hero during the Meuse-Argonne Offensive of 1918, picking off a line of Germans "like a flock of turkeys" and capturing, with the help of seven other men, 132 of the enemy. He returns to the United States to be smothered in accolades—the Congressional Medal of Honor, a ticker tape parade, the key to the city of New York, and a room in the Waldorf Astoria, the latter a tribute from Tennessee Representative, Cordell Hull (who became F.D.R.'s secretary of state). Of all the honors bestowed upon him, York is most touched by the presence of his mother's photograph in his hotel room and later by Hull's thoughtfulness in placing a long distance call to his mother in Tennessee. As he cautiously speaks on this "weird instrument," a most appealing and convincing Gary Cooper persuades the audience that neither York's war experience nor his brush with fame has changed him. He remains an unassuming, gawky boy, loyal to the simple values he absorbed while growing up in an impoverished family in a small American town. Although flooded with requests, York eschews his opportunities for wealth and renown in the city and returns to the Tennessee mountains. What he did in France, he declares, was "not for buying or selling."

York's homecoming is a scene of joyful confusion; a local band, a crowd of well-wishers, the pastor and York's family and sweetheart turn out to greet the hero. As York climbs off the train, he is swamped by celebrants whom he tries to placate while his eyes search the crowd for his mother. While York weaves his way toward her, the camera shifts back and forth, showing the relief, anguish, and happiness that flicker over both their faces. "Ma, I'm back," Alvin says. "I'm right glad, son," Mother York replies.

Gracie then claims York's attention, as befits the sweetheart who has waited faithfully through the war. Alvin's intentions remain honorable; he apologetically explains to Gracie that the war has set him back and that they will have to wait until he can obtain the proper parcel of land to be married. Gracie insists with gentle determination "I'm expecting my husband to love me. I reckon the good Lord will take care of the rest."

Thus Alvin York's odyssey ends. He returns, a proven man of the world who nevertheless rejects its sophistication for the simple pleasure of close-to-the-earth family living in his religious farming community. Such humility is, of course, rewarded. As the film ends, the York family reveals Tennessee's tribute to Alvin—a "House and Garden" farmhouse built on the section of land Alvin had worked so arduously to own. As the happy strains of the romantic theme are heard, Alvin and Gracie run toward their new home, free of both worldly and spiritual cares.

At first glance, the popular film biography of Alvin York appears to offer little of worth to the historian of American women. Throughout the movie, the camera loyally follows Gary Cooper as he reenacts the exploits of the famous sergeant. In the major action portions of the film—Alvin's "hell-raisin," the shooting competition where York's prowess with a rifle is affirmed, the war scenes in France—women are spectators or shadowy impressions in men's minds. And during York's dramatic moment of choice, his companions are his dog and two books.

An interpretation based on these highlights of *Sergeant York* would lead easily to a view of women as marginal characters in a society at war. Since film reviewers generally praised the top money-making film of 1941 as a "documentary description . . . of the South's mountainfolk," one may assume that the female characters in *Sergeant York* met the popular expectations attached to rural heroines in a wartime crisis. The accuracy of Margaret Wycherly's and Joan Leslie's portrayals of the genuine Mother York and Gracie was not addressed by critics, even though Gary Cooper's Alvin York was described as "a completely persuasive characterization."[6]

Film reviewers' lack of concern for the authenticity of women's roles in *Sergeant York* raises some interesting questions. Either the characters were considered too unimportant to notice (although the actresses were complimented for their fine performances), or public perceptions dictated that a part of women's charm lay in their contentment to be passive bystanders in a nation at war. The latter view, while apparently acceptable to audiences in 1941, revealed a marked insensitivity to historical reality. Since no record exists of Gracie's or Mother York's reactions to their screen portrayals, the accuracy of their images cannot be firmly ascertained—but speculation is possible. For women of their movie time (approximately 1912–1920), they were presented as remarkably unaffected by the issues that commanded the attention of so many of their sex. Although perceived as a documentary of the World War I period, *Sergeant York* distorted the reality of females' lives considerably. What, then, were the obvious omissions in this acclaimed film's historical picture of women?

Most striking, to this analyst, is *Sergeant York's* lack of attention to females' active participation in the Great War effort. Some one and one-half million women joined the labor force during World War I, and millions of others "knitted their bit" or performed other volunteer services. Such an oversight—in a popular film lauded as "the strongest (of the pre-World War II films) preaching the necessity for taking up arms in the nation's defense," suggests that a full-scale use of women in the imminent war against the Axis powers was only a remote possibility to most Americans in 1941. War was still considered a male domain, so thoroughly separate from women's spheres that women could neither understand the politics involved nor give advice to troubled men confronting hard decisions. According to Hawks' film, popular attitudes in 1941 supported the notion that women's obligations during war remained a different sort. Their major patriotic response was to let their men go, gracefully, accepting the war condition as a necessary one. And, then, they were required, in the words of a favorite song, to "Keep the Home Fires Burning."[7]

In the film *Sergeant York* both Mother York and Gracie handle these societal demands with ease. They do not fuss with Alvin when he decides that killing is, after all, justifiable, even if their religious convictions differ from his. And Mother York manages, during the war years, to "grow corn out of rocks" without Alvin's help. Both women wait patiently for York's return, praying for his survival and never questioning the reasons for his participation—or their country's—in the war.

This image of women seemingly fitted with the popular folklore of theater-goers in 1941; certainly one finds no suggestion of discontent with women's portrayals in reviewers' or film historians' critiques of *Sergeant York*. Yet it hardly mirrored the historical realities of the World War I era, and this omission implies that an important segment of women's history had been lost in the inter-war years.[8]

The period of the Great War was actually a time of intense dispute over "woman's place" in American society. A vocal minority of women no longer exhibited the quiet acceptance exemplified by Mother York and Gracie, particularly on the issues of pacifism and war. Anne Martin, an especially outspoken organizer for the Woman's Party in Nevada, roundly attacked the Wilson Administration for its militarism as early as 1916. "Even the claim that he kept us out of war is absurd," she wrote in a letter to an acquaintance. "He gave Germany every chance to fight us

. . . [and] the only place where Wilson could get us to go to war, he did; that is with Mexico."[9]

While many participants of the women's movement did not share Martin's dislike of Wilson or her pacifism, they did insist on an active public role for American females. Although the women characters in *Sergeant York* appeared uninterested or mystified by political issues, suffrage for women actually occupied a predominant spot on the public agenda at the time of their movie lives, and few persons in the country were without opinions on the subject. Even the remote environs of Tennessee were not protected from the political struggle. The legislature of the Yorks' home state gave the final ratification to the 19th Amendment, placing it securely in the Constitution, and a key vote was cast by Harry Burn, a 24-year-old representative from rural East Tennessee whose mother, an ardent suffragist, had cabled him "to be a good boy. And vote for suffrage. . . ."[10]

The idea of women's suffrage had been gaining strength in the public imagination a decade before Woodrow Wilson called for a Declaration of War against Germany, the same time period (in *Sergeant York*) in which Gracie and Mother York had concentrated on supporting Alvin in his struggle for bottomland. The apolitical women in *Sergeant York* were cast from a different mold than the determined women (and men) who had organized repeated referenda at the state level, achieving their goal of enfranchisement in Washington (1910) and California (1911), but swallowing defeat in Michigan, Ohio, and Wisconsin. Setbacks at the state level prompted an energetic campaign for a federal law, and by 1916, both the National American Woman's Suffrage Association and the brash, newly-formed Woman's Party were agitating for passage of the Susan B. Anthony Amendment.[11]

Getting the vote was only one priority on the agenda of many feminists. The generation of educated young women who reached adulthood in the era of Progressive reform did not limit themselves to suffrage parades and lobbies; they also worked in settlement houses, encouraged labor unions, and occasionally spoke for racial justice. Those who did not align themselves with the phalanxes of reform found other ways to express their discontent with traditional ideas of women's roles. The new woman or flapper of the 1920s had predecessors in the pre-war years. Guardians of the old ways worried over fast girls who flirted outrageously and danced with strange men before and during World War I.[12]

But achieving suffrage was the most cohesive issue among women reformers, partly because anti-suffragists had rallied both money and voices in a strong effort to defeat the 19th Amendment. The ranks of the opposition included many women who, ironically, took a public stand on a political issue to avoid assuming that role in the future. While it is easier to imagine Mother York and Gracie at an anti-feminist gathering in their local church than a suffrage parade in the state capital, *Sergeant York* conveys no sense of them as persons who had any interests at all in such issues. In rural America, the film implies, matters outside the home and church were strictly men's business.[13]

Interestingly, the very idea of definitive male and female domains was being questioned most severely by radical feminists in the era before World War I. And, in the active debate over women's and men's places, even the home—the environ that Gracie and Mother York automatically accepted as their destiny—was not sacrosanct. One of the eminent theoreticians of the early twentieth-century women's movement, Charlotte Perkins Gilman, delivered an ardent attack on the institution. In Gilman's view, individual family units, centered around a wife/mother figure, were inefficient and debilitating. Society's living arrangements isolated women, cheating the nation of their resources and talents. "Science, art, government, education, industry—" she wrote, "the home is the cradle of them all, and the grave if they stay in it."[14]

The public dialogue on the woman question did not fade when America joined the Allied effort to destroy the "Huns." While the women characters in *Sergeant York* stoically accepted the war, militant suffragists picketed the White House, carrying placards that urged President Wilson to remember, "Democracy Begins At Home." Less insistent feminists supported the war effort, but they also demanded public recognition of the expertise shown by women who assumed formerly male jobs, whether those female replacements operated elevators, manufactured steel plates, or served on government war committees. And millions of women, suffragists and anti-suffragists, performed volunteer services during the war— making surgical dressings, knitting socks for soldiers, feeding guardsmen, processing paper work, and writing letters to lonely soldiers abroad.[15]

Yet *Sergeant York* included no allusions to this segment of women's history. Such an omission speaks quite clearly to the public consciousness of 1941. The earlier struggles to expand Americans' perceptions of women's domains had faltered during the inter-war years, and the traditional roles of women—wife, mother, and sweetheart—were once again ascendant in the public mind.

The rural setting of the film added a touch of authenticity and nostalgia to the film's portrayal of women. Whatever the realities of pioneer life, in American folklore the females and males most unaffected by unsettling quarrels over sexual roles were those who tackled difficult land in remote areas. The mountains of Tennessee evoked the pioneer spirit, and the characters in *Sergeant York* preserved the American mythology of the valued old ways in which families interacted in the days before cities and technology rudely changed the nation's landscape and the appointed place of females in the social hierarchy.[16]

Within this context, the images of Mother York and Gracie assume a different complexion. There was no hint, in their characterizations, of the new woman of the twentieth century who found "children, kitchen, church" to be a limiting, even debilitating sphere. Their movie reflections did suggest, however, the attributes that Americans prized in the traditional culture of women, even on the verge of a war that would severely challenge the attitudes that bolstered women's confinement to them.

What then, was the nature of women's culture according to *Sergeant York*? In the nineteenth century, Elizabeth Cady Stanton described woman's portion as "wife, mother, housekeeper, physician, and spiritual guide."[17] This definition holds for women's lot in Howard Hawks' film, with a special twist on the last designation. The women in this much-viewed movie were spiritual guides increased several decibels. Although the action of the picture revolved around the title character, the supportive roles of mother and sweetheart were used to confirm York's successes and failures. If the women in York's life were pleased with him, then God and society would also grant recognition; if a worried frown creased Mother York's or Gracie's face, then societal disapproval was not far behind.

Thus *Sergeant York* implied that women served as society's moral judges or arbiters. An important part of women's culture was to evaluate human behavior, assessing family members' or suitors' strengths and weaknesses and establishing acceptable standards of conduct for them. Both Mother York and Gracie conveyed a sense of pride in their ability to fulfill this role. They both entertained great hopes for the intrepid Alvin, and they actively influenced him to become an aggressive bread-winner and a kind and stable family man. Moreover, ultimate purpose in York's life came from the pathway they had suggested, conversion to religion.

As moral arbiters, the women in the popular 1941 film meted out both approval and punishment. The value of York's exhausting days behind the plow was verified by a kiss from Gracie and his mother's prayerful concern. On the other hand, his "hell-raisin" earned him a bucket of water in the face and rivals for Gracie's affection. Significantly, Alvin accepted both his mother's and sweetheart's judgement of him. According to *Sergeant York*, both males and females expected women to provide the moral basis for the family, much as men fulfilled a breadwinning role. Wives and mothers concerned themselves with the harmonious interaction of family members, soliciting behavior from their men and children that reflected religious constancy and social responsibility. Deviant conduct was understood, but did not go unpunished.

Moral judgements were only one aspect of women's work. In the farm-based economy depicted in the film, women's days were busy with practical, day-to-day considerations, taking care of children, growing and processing food, placing nutritious meals on the table, keeping a home in order, and worrying about the economic survival of the farm. The movie intimated that these tasks were demanding ones that required women's full energies and talents—and also elicited community respect.

The more clearly developed woman figure in the film, the widowed Mother York, received special esteem for her competence in keeping her family together and eking out a living from the tired soil of the Tennessee mountains. Although the visual footage of Mother York was limited, she was a commanding presence in the motion picture, worrying over her children (and receiving their respect and love in return) and relying upon God, her feelings and the wisdom of past family history to face crises.[18] Since Mother York emerged as a heroine, it is a safe assumption that audiences of 1941 found her a meaningful reflector of women's work. Both she, and her younger version, Gracie, seemed content with their domains. When events occurred outside Mother York's sphere of under-standing—war, for example—she relied on her faith to sustain her. Her answer to her daughter's question, "Ma, what are they a fightin' for?" "I don't rightly know, child," clearly showed that Mother York found the intellectual issues of democracy and freedom outside her scope; political dilemmas raised by warfare could be tolerated only by accepting God's will.

Mother York's role as family matriarch was established firmly at the beginning of *Sergeant York*, the result of a distant marriage, child-bearing, and the unfortunate loss of her husband. Gracie's choices had not yet been made, although her major decision would be whom she would marry, and other options were not presented. The film idealized a period of comfortable order in rural American society where sexual roles were concerned. A woman's place was to select a provider carefully while she was young and pretty, and thereafter, her function was to care for the man she had chosen, helping him to achieve economic security and nur-turing the children to whom she gave birth. Gracie's work, therefore, was to guide the process of courtship, determining York's readiness for mar-riage, and insuring that he meet her demands in order to win her. Although the ending of the film suggested that Gracie's only criterion for marriage was a husband who would love her, the audience was aware of the ma-terial comforts that York's military feats had brought him; thus Gracie's gamble was slight, for God (or the Tennessee government) had already provided.

The romantic resolution in *Sergeant York* was only one component of the movie's happy ending. The war was over, the enemy was defeated, Alvin had gained a reputation as the man who could knock off the "whole sauerkraut army" and the York family was reunited.[19] Just as Alvin's heroism in France had earned him public acclaim, Mother York's and Gracie's proper behavior during the war years—being supportive but unobtrusive figures—had resulted in their prayers being answered. After the Armistice, York returned to the Valley of the Three Forks of the Wolf, satisfied to bypass fame and affluence for the rewards of marriage and close family ties. And York's return enabled his mother and eventual wife to remain contented with traditional women's work, giving full time to the jobs of moral arbiter and family and household chieftains.

Although the historian of American women might wish for a "Mother York" or "Gracie" film that probed the private moments of decision in a woman's life, *Sergeant York* conveyed a reasonable glimpse of Americans' perceptions of rural women's culture on the eve of World War II. Popular folklore accepted the importance of these women's work without question. The sentimental moments of the movie indicated that the day-to-day activities of females were ones that sustained family life and gave purpose to existence. During war, the type of stability represented by women assumed new dimensions. While men fought wars of conscience or trenches, women were caretakers of society's most basic institutions. In 1941 competence in such a role suggested the making of a heroine.

The rural heroines in *Sergeant York* were nostalgic but meaningful characters. They spoke to the deep roots of sexual assuredness in American society. But they were not the only images of women that flashed across the screen in 1941. The new woman, whose history was non-existent in the popular biography of Alvin York, appeared in other box-office hits of the same year. The major woman character in Frank Capra's *Meet John Doe* offered a different—and startlingly contrasting—view of female capability.[20]

Meet John Doe (Warner Brothers, 1941)

Meet John Doe (Warner Brothers, 1941) was one of a small group of pre-war films vaguely designed to alert Americans to the dangers of internal fascism. This genre of movie did not appear in theaters until the spring of 1939 when, Lewis Jacobs wrote, *Confessions of a Nazi Spy* "documented the spread of Nazi ideology in the United States and bluntly warned against a fascist Fifth Column." Although some commentators congratulated the producers of the 1939 feature for exposing long overdue issues, other Americans supported the stance of Senator Burton K. Wheeler of Montana, who insisted that movies had become "gigantic engines of propaganda . . . designed to drug the reason of the American people."[21]

Faced with the same division in the body politic that haunted Franklin D. Roosevelt and his administrators, profit-minded Hollywood producers chose to straddle a thin line. From 1939 to 1941 films concerned with dictators, militarism, and subjugated peoples had a foreign or fantasy setting, and they were heavily counterbalanced in theaters with escapist movies of the romance, comedy, or adventure type.[22]

Meet John Doe, director Frank Capra's and screenwriter Robert Riskin's first independent production under a Warner Brothers' umbrella, reflected the ambiguity of these pre-war attitudes in the United States. The villains in the movie were obviously fascists to the observant American, but no labels were used. And, within the film's plot, traditional American values (based on Christianity and community involvement) provided the antidote to subversive activities, although the cure was not simple, and determination and commitment were required to squelch the enemy.

John Doe, played by Americans' favorite hero of 1941, Gary Cooper, was ostensibly the figure behind whom people rallied in the American struggle to prevent a capitalist dictatorship. But another person actually provided the ideas and energy for the John Doe Movement in the film. An urban heroine, Ann Mitchell (Barbara Stanwyck), "the newspaper girl, with her breezy column, her embroilment in current events," furnished important ingredients in the fight against internal fascism, as the story of *Meet John Doe* revealed.[23]

Meet John Doe, the last of Frank Capra's pre-World War II tributes to the common man, was a gripping melodrama which explored the reactions of Americans to an internal fascist threat.[24] In the course of the motion picture, corrupt politicians, businessmen, and union leaders were exposed, and average people were shown to be the skilled champions of democracy. Under Capra's direction, the camera was relentless and captivating, illuminating segments of American society with artful finesse: the bustling clamor in the offices of a large urban newspaper; the opulent castles of the very rich; the poverty, despair and stubborn hope in hobo camps; the quiet simplicity of ordinary American homes; and huge crowds of fearful people, desperately seeking affirmation of themselves in troubled times.

The beginning scene of the film establishes the perilous nature of those times. As the camera cuts swiftly from a nursery of squalling babies to a chisel removing the word "free" from a massive stone building that housed a newspaper, the viewers are visually persuaded that the new generation is in danger of losing its birthright. And, as the drama of the movie unfolds, the evil forces that menace the American way of life are revealed, and the audience is offered methods for combating fascism and preserving traditional American freedoms.

Bigness—the growth of large, impersonal institutions—is the first threat to the American mode of living to be exposed in *Meet John Doe*. *The Free Bulletin*, a newspaper that embodied small town values such as compassionate interest in its employees, has been swept into the orbit of a huge newspaper chain, controlled by the mysterious and sinister D. B. Norton (Edward Arnold). As a result of the merger, *The Free Bulletin* has become *The New Bulletin*, "a streamlined newspaper for a streamlined era," and several journalists are dismissed. The collapse of values such as reverence for age and respect for employees' seniority is conveyed when an arrogant message boy reveals their fate to some old-timers; figuratively slitting his throat with his finger, the boy gleefully follows this gesture with an "out" thumb signal, notifying several loyal reporters of the end of their tenure.

Pert, intelligent, and articulate Ann Mitchell (Barbara Stanwyck) is among those who lose their jobs in the new reorganization. Dismayed and frightened, the aspiring young newspaperwoman pleads with her editor, Connell (James Gleason), to reinstate her, for she is the only breadwinner in her fatherless family, providing support for her mother and two sisters. When Connell curtly denies her request, claiming that he has no power to intercede, the energetic Mitchell determines to fight back, and she does so by writing an angry "John Doe" letter of protest in place of her usual "lavender and lace" column on the women's page. Ignoring the sensible advice of her male colleagues (who are concerned with the ethics of publishing a fictitious letter), Mitchell rapidly types her missive and submits it directly to the press room. The letter contains an angry complaint about the state of civilization—Mitchell's "John Doe" insists that Americans have become victims of overpowering forces. Death is better than such a life, the imaginary Doe concludes, and accordingly, the letter ends with Doe's threat to commit suicide at the end of the year.

Thus John Doe is born, the brain-child of an ambitious, tough newspaperwoman who refuses to accept the loss of her job passively. The letter's publication provokes an amazing response. Mitchell's cry of outrage in *Meet John Doe* seemingly reflects the feelings of thousands of lost

Americans, and even the mayor and governor call *The New Bulletin* to ask "Who is John Doe?"

The answer to this question poses severe problems to editor Connell, who angrily counsels Mitchell to "go on out and get married and have a lot of babies but stay out of the newspaper business." Mitchell ignores this advice also, competing with her boss's wrath by suggesting a resolution based on duplicity but shrewdly calculated to boost circulation: why not hire a John Doe? When a dozen men show up claiming to be the bogus author of Ann's column, Connell relents. Fearing for his own job if he has to admit that his newspaper has perpetrated a hoax, Connell accepts Mitchell's idea, reinstating her on *The New Bulletin* staff and giving her a bonus. As the person in charge of the John Doe story, Mitchell now has new opportunities for wealth, influence, and personal corruption.

The task of finding a John Doe is easily accomplished when Gary Cooper appears on the scene in the person of an injured baseball pitcher, "Long John" Willoughby, who cannot afford medical treatment. Thin, ragged, and fainting from hunger, Willoughby is the perfect candidate for the dispirited John Doe who has vowed in Mitchell's letter to leap from City Hall on Christmas Day in protest to the state of civilization. Despite the opposition of his side-kick, the Colonel (Walter Brennan), Long John agrees to *The New Bulletin*'s terms: he will impersonate John Doe in exchange for the operation his arm requires and a ticket out of town before December 25th.

While *The New Bulletin* is flooded with letters which echo John Doe's vague complaints, Mitchell cleverly builds suspense regarding the enigmatic hero, keeping him sequestered in a hotel room (the most luxurious environment that hoboes Willoughby and the Colonel have experienced). Eventually the irate citizenry, newly aware of its own strength, takes to the streets to protest the ineptitude of its political leaders. Friendliness, neighborly love, and concern for one's fellow persons are touted as the values that will end the creeping success of the impersonal bureaucracies that make victims of the common people. As John Doe Clubs form, politicians are excluded, and Americans are shown competently handling their problems by means of direct democracy in small community centers.

The "smoke-filled room" has not vanished from the American scene, however. A presence more sinister than bungling politicians now looms on the screen in *Meet John Doe*. As Ann Mitchell answers a summons to his estate, fascist D. B. Norton is seen astride a sleek horse, reviewing his personal motorcycle corps as they glide through precise military maneuvers. Undaunted by this display of police power, the ambitious Mitchell succumbs to Norton's assurances of future wealth and security and agrees to help further D. B.'s political aspirations. "You will be pulling the strings [of the John Doe Movement]," she guarantees, and proceeds to manipulate Willoughby into giving a radio speech.

Ann Mitchell is, of course, only a misguided villain. Thus the speech she writes for John Doe's radio premiere is full of homespun American truths, taken mostly from the diary of her father, a doctor devoted to kindness rather than the accumulation of material goods. Further inspiration comes from Ann's mother, a sweet and generous woman who places altruism before practical considerations, constantly buying groceries for others even when her family has little food of its own. In a beautifully developed scene, a nervous Willoughby stands before the radio microphone, the script quivering, and delivers his introductory message to Americans—in essence, "Wake up, all you 'John Does!' " Immediately afterward, despite a warm congratulatory hug from Mitchell, Long John bolts, escaping back to hobo land with the Colonel, who has continually warned him against involvement with the established world of women, furniture, and controlled behavior.

Long John's attempt to escape is fruitless, however, for the hopes and aspirations his speech has kindled in the hearts of his fellow "John Does" is too powerful to ignore. As he embarks on a nationwide tour, relying on Ann for his speeches, Willoughby's baseball pitcher-hobo identity blurs, and he *becomes* "John Doe"—the American who "has been hungry or wanting something most of his life." Mitchell also changes as she accompanies John Doe through the small towns of the United States, and as the affection between them assumes romantic proportions, Mitchell begins to feel guilty about her pact with Norton.

Ann's fear that she has made the wrong choice in supporting D. B. Norton is resoundingly verified in the next scenes. As one of the select guests at Norton's ostentatious dinner party (where Mitchell finds a fur coat and diamond bracelet waiting for her), Ann listens with horror to D. B.'s plans. Carefully cleaning his glasses throughout the recital, Norton explains that the John Doe Movement (now meeting in national convention) will become his vehicle to take over the apparatus of government in the United States. The support D. B. has carefully engineered in the business and labor communities is visually presented in the obsequious actions of his dinner companions who are leading spokesmen of those groups.

As Mitchell questions Norton in her tough journalist manner (she is the only woman at the table and the sole person to challenge Norton), the camera shifts to a drunken editor Connell who has managed to corner John Doe and convince him of his need to look over the speech written for his delivery at the National John Doe Convention. Connell, shorn of his hard shell by several shots of bourbon, reminisces about World War I— he had been in the same unit as his father and had witnessed his death— eventually ending his rambling by confessing his deep affection for de- mocracy and the "Star-Spangled Banner." Impressed, Willoughby reads the speech which was to have catapulted Norton to national acclaim. Finally realizing his naïve involvement in a conspiracy, Long John rushes to Norton's estate to confront Mitchell and the scheming fascist.

John Doe's moment of revelation is quixotic and ineffectual. Like Ann Mitchell's arguments, his protests against Norton's plot are circum- scribed by the latter's planning. Overwhelmed by Norton's thugs when he tries to confront the movie's villain, Long John staggers to the con- vention, where he tries to warn his followers of Norton's scheme.

Unfortunately, D. B.'s storm troopers have preceded him to the rain-drenched coliseum filled with singing, optimistic patriots. As John Doe enters, Norton's thugs are carrying out a well-formed plan, distrib- uting pamphlets that reveal the truth of Willoughby's origin, sabotaging the public address system to prevent Long John from being heard, and activating pre-planned riots to create confusion. As the crowd turns hos- tile and ugly, John Doe is coaxed away by his loyal friend, the Colonel, while Mitchell is prevented from reaching him by Norton's henchmen. Repudiating her connections with Norton, Mitchell thinks only of Wil- loughby/Doe: "He was so all alone," she weeps, "I should have been with him."

The final scene of *Meet John Doe* occurs months later on a snowy, tense Christmas Eve in the tower atop City Hall.[25] In the intervening time since the abortive convention, Willoughby has not been seen, and Ann Mitchell, dispirited and exhausted, has fallen ill. Meanwhile, as the masses of peo- ple who had supported the John Doe Movement retreat into their private shells, Norton has continued the manipulative tactics which he still hopes will place him in control of the federal government. As the snow falls softly on Christmas Eve, Ann leaves her sick bed to join the few others— editor Connell, Norton and his bodyguards, the Colonel—who wait to see if Long John will try to vindicate John Doe by leaping from City Hall as the first letter had threatened.

This is, of course, the courageous Long John Willoughby's inten- tion. The Movement has come to mean more to him than his life, and if his suicide will rekindle faith in the ideas of neighborly love, personal alertness to evil, and a commitment to the Golden Rule, then he is a willing sacrifice. Ann Mitchell cries hysterically, pleading her love for him as reason enough not to commit suicide, but John Doe is adamant—until the members of the first John Doe Club appear. Shy and thoughtful Americans, they explain how their lives have been enriched by this non-political movement, and they persuade Willoughby that all their country-men need to hear the message from him—personally. A common cause among ordinary people can defeat even fascist D. B. Norton, the audience learns, and as John Doe, Ann Mitchell and the representative good Amer-icans leave City Hall, smiling and determined, the forces menacing Amer-ican society are seen to have met their match.[26]

The movie-going public who filtered into theaters in 1941 to see *Meet John Doe* would have had few problems identifying the society portrayed in the film. The fashions of both men and women, the models of auto-mobiles, the state of newspaper and radio technology, street scenes, and the interiors of wealthy or simple homes reflected contemporary Ameri-can society. The problems supposedly straining the nation to a point of vulnerability to *coups d'etat* were also recognizable as pressures left over from the thirties: economic depression which displaced solid, middle-class Americans and begat clusters of roving bums; the growth of large, impersonal bureaucracies; an increasing concentration of wealth and power in an upper class who appeared to profit from the nation's economic woes.[27] In the course of explaining society's problems, the film exposed villains in homegrown American institutions—city, state, and national political organizations, business corporations, labor unions—and featured small community meetings and neighborly interaction among people as the ultimate security of the democratic system. The motion picture cast a sentimental and loving eye on the common person, but it also carried a warning that naivete was dangerous and could make dupes of even well-meaning people. "Wake up, John Doe," sounded an alarm to Americans that their traditional freedoms could be preserved only by alert and co-operative action.[28]

In this endeavor to rescue the nation, an energetic and capable ca-reer woman played an important role. Ann Mitchell, portrayed by young, blond, and vivacious Barbara Stanwyck, was the prime mover in the John Doe story, articulating the frustrations of the forgotten masses, and plac-ing in motion a movement to return power to the people. Although she became involved in Norton's manipulations, Mitchell was not alone. Her crusty editor, Connell, with years of experience in the competitive news-paper world, also supported the fascist through most of the film.

Mitchell's background and motivation for a career in journalism were explained early in the motion picture. A product of a middle-class family, she had eschewed the traditional domains of women not for ful-fillment of her potential but because of economic necessity. Her kind doctor-father had died, leaving the family without a breadwinner, and Ann, the oldest child, assumed that function, allowing her mother and two sisters to continue their supportive roles in the family and community. As a part of the competitive, male business world, Ann Mitchell adopted the values and behavior deemed necessary for wealth and success—she schemed, employed trickery, and was consistently aggressive in articulating her views.[29] She was accepted in the newspaper business as an equal colleague for she was working for the same reason as her male colleagues—earning a livelihood and supporting others. Within the context of the film Stanwyck as Mitchell exuded volatile energy; she was as pushy as any man and more ambitious than most. Newly arrived to the newspaper game, she possessed few of the scruples of conservative professionalism and little fear of the extant authoritarian hierarchy. Mitchell used her witty, sharp tongue and exceptional writing skills to outmaneuver her editor—not just to keep her job but to gain a promotion. The duplicity she relied on was not encouraged by her male colleagues, but her prowess was admired and she was shown to have received her advances through her ingenuity in creating a story rather than a resort to feminine wiles.

In fact, there were few instances in *Meet John Doe* in which Mitchell's femininity was stressed. Although she was often the only woman in male-dominated scenes, she behaved and thought as her companions, thus mitigating any sense of uniqueness. Long John's partner, the pessimistic Colonel, saw Mitchell's attractiveness as part of the bait which kept Willoughby a participant in the newspaper hoax, but the faith of common people in the movement was the final source of Doe's commitment. Mitchell's active presence in the scheme added sexual tension and the possibility of romance, for few Hollywood films would be considered complete without some variation of the mating game. Yet, when Mitchell attempted to assume a traditional woman's role, such as moral arbiter, she was unsuccessful. In the scene at D. B. Norton's mansion when the fascist revealed his sinister plans, Mitchell's protests were fruitless. The film suggested that Mitchell, who had been an integral partner in the plotting, was too tainted by corruption to be a convincing umpire. By entering the male sphere, she had forfeited woman's traditional rights to masculine courtesy and to the assumed higher morality of society's gentler sex.

The romance between John Doe and Ann Mitchell further illustrated the extent to which sexual roles had become ambiguous in a complex, urban society. Willoughby was clearly unacceptable as a mate when he first appeared in his poverty-stricken, dishevelled state. Mitchell, the established one of the twosome, raised him to national prominence, only to find herself rejected for her manipulative tactics. John Doe was the naive innocent in this case, and Mitchell was the person who had to be purified through suffering before she would be worthy of him. The 1941 film implied that, in urban America, sexual distinctions had blurred considerably from the rural, agricultural times evoked in *Sergeant York*. In *Meet John Doe*, a woman was a breadwinner whose job claimed her first attention, and the male star was unworldly and vulnerable.[30]

Of course, John Doe and Ann Mitchell were paired at the end of the film, the personification of the motion picture's message that love, caring and involvement could conquer even fascist enemies. Their mating, however, was not the result of Mitchell's renunciation of her career (such a personal issue would have appeared petty in the dramatic sweep of the film's last moments) but the product of their mutual pledge to forget past errors by "taking stock in American optimism" and reorganizing the John Doe Movement.[31] The motion picture suggested that women must be as involved as men in combating internal threats to national security, and the film was distinctly silent in portraying women's gifts as different from those of men in this endeavor.

Despite Mitchell's prominent role in *Meet John Doe*, the title and focus of the film reflected the continued public perception that only a man could be the spokesperson for the common people. The real John Doe, Ann Mitchell, remained behind the scenes, employing her considerable talents writing speeches and organizing a grass roots' movement. Mitchell was more than a paid helpmate, however. She was the brains behind the movement—the person close enough to the pulse of the land to sense Americans' frustrations and hopes. She was defeated when she succumbed to false gods—money and recognition—and she was rescued by a painful renunciation of her drive for individualistic success. Ann Mitchell's experiences embodied the moral lesson of the film. In the America visualized in *Meet John Doe*, women active in the marketplace faced the same problems and temptations as their male counterparts, and they resolved their dilemmas with no greater ease and no lesser struggle. Caught in the Horatio Alger myths of their past, American men and women could be complaisant targets for fascism in a divided world that required unity and collective action.

Sergeant York and *Meet John Doe* were the only dramatic best sellers of 1941 to consider either internal or external threats to the American way of life.[32] Other films appeared on this theme, of course. Comedies such as *Caught in the Draft*, starring Bob Hope, and *Buck Privates*, an Abbott and Costello vehicle, were popular hits while critics acclaimed serious anti-Nazi movies such as *Man Hunt* and *The Great Dictator*. Judging from money paid at the box-office, however, Americans were reluctant to confront the possibility of involvement in the war against the fascists and they were equally unwilling to label enemies in their home territory. Before the "Day of Infamy" at Pearl Harbor, Americans preferred their war preparation in historical, vague doses.

Both *Sergeant York* and *Meet John Doe* filled this prescription. Capra's film carried reassurances to movie patrons that fascism would not happen here, while Alvin York's biography convincingly showed that Americans could handle an enemy "over there" when necessary. Neither film suggested that war might rupture the social fabric at home, threatening old-time values and patterns of living rather than strengthening them. And the realities of torn limbs and sudden death in combat were not emphasized in *Sergeant York*. Critics noted, in fact, that the battle scenes in the top-grossing movie took up "comparatively little footage," resulting in a picture that was "amazingly little a war film, not at all . . . another of those chronicles of trench warfare."[33] Apparently, in 1941, Americans were not willing to spend money to encourage war fever or to think about war's effect on the home front.

Neither were Americans eager to recapture, according to these popular films, the old days of World War I when women left their homes to work in war industries or march in suffrage parades. If a time of crisis should occur, *Sergeant York* implied, then the old folklore of rural Americans was best—women's work lay in preserving marriage, home, church, and the family. There was dignity and importance in such work, even if the camera did not elucidate it.

Yet, in 1941, Rosie the Riveter could have been at least a gleam in an artist's eye. As *Meet John Doe* illustrated, the working woman of intelligence and competence had become a recognized female in American thought. The new woman, born of the cities, the Progressive Feminist Movement, and the hard times of depression America, had also entered American folklore.

Both images were strong and persuasive, but they did not project a total dichotomy. The women in *Sergeant York* and *Meet John Doe* had a common bond—the roots of their lives lay in their relationships with men and their families, and in a larger context, in understanding people's motives and behaviors. While Mother York and Gracie limited their interest and arts in guidance to traditional women's spheres, venturing no comments on the state of the nation or the conduct of people outside their community, Ann Mitchell's job as a newspaperwoman thrust her into a national forum. In *Meet John Doe*, this city-bred survivor's uniqueness lay in her willingness to write what was, according to the movie, formerly considered unprintable—the genuine despairs and hopes felt by ordinary Americans.

Thus, on the eve of World War II, popular mythology appeared to place both rural and urban women in charge of human relationships in American society. While the females in York's life handled their local obligations with ease, Ann Mitchell's experiences suggested that acting in a public forum was not simple. *Meet John Doe* carried overtones of the old anti-suffragist prophecy—once women trailed "their skirts in the muck and mire of . . . politics," they forfeited their right to chivalry (a type of male behavior that ennobled society) and weakened their position as guardians of American culture.[34]

The outlines of women's work as caretakers and arbiters can only be inferred from these popular pre-war movies. Marriage, home, sexuality, family, and church were considered private domains at that time, sacrosanct from public view.[35] Still, Mother York's role as a wise and judicious matriarch was easily readable and Gracie's preparation for the same function was apparent. Ann Mitchell's pathway was more torturous. The loss of a family breadwinner had forced her into a traditional male role, and the consequent splitting of her attention had severe ramifications. While Mitchell's accomplishments appeared greater than Mother York's or Gracie's, *Meet John Doe* suggested that her suffering was also more dramatic. In contrast to the new woman's lot, the old ways of rural America seemed secure and comprehensible.

Yet the public decision was in Ann Mitchell's favor if the emphases of these two films can be believed. Despite the adherence to the folklore regarding women's traditional place that dominated *Sergeant York* and seeped into *Meet John Doe*, Ann Mitchell emerged as the most dynamic female characterization in these two pre-World War II films. The camera followed her into her private life, showing her working on her speeches (that John Doe would parrot) in the same manner that the camera trailed Sergeant York onto his mountaintop. And, while the audience was not privy to Mother York's or Gracie's private agonies, *Meet John Doe* included Ann Mitchell's moments of decision.

Evidently, in 1941, women's culture was perceived as important—but untouchable or uninteresting. The real shootable cinema action occurred outside feminine spheres. Significantly, the bombs at Pearl Harbor would shift Americans' interest. After the United States became a protagonist in the "People's War," the effects of war on the home front—and on women's domains—became more important to the movie-going public.

The result was a different genre of motion picture—one dubbed the "woman's film" by critics. The first major war movie in this genre was Metro-Goldwyn-Mayer's "almost impossible feat, a great war picture that photographs the inner meaning . . . of World War II"—*Mrs. Miniver* (1942).[36]

The Impact of War on Women's Domains: An Ally's Home Front

Mrs. Miniver (Metro-Goldwyn-Mayer, 1942)

Once President Franklin D. Roosevelt had called for a Declaration of War against Japan, and Germany had backed up its Asian ally by numbering the United States among Nazi enemies, Americans tried to prepare themselves for a war of several years' duration.[1] Faced with a crisis that demanded new understanding and approaches, Americans relied upon movies for the emotional overtones missing from radio bulletins, government directives, or newspaper accounts. Speaking before the Academy of Motion Picture Arts and Sciences in early 1943, Lowell Mellett, chief of the Bureau of Motion Pictures (an agency in the Office of War Information) addressed this function of films. "The motion picture is largely an emotional art," Mellett explained. "Motion picture artists devote themselves to making people laugh and cry, as well as think. They devote themselves to making people feel. That is the art of motion pictures."[2]

Director William Wyler's epic, *Mrs. Miniver*, seemed tailor-made to fill this need. Set in a sympathetic ally's country, England, and spanning the years from 1939 to 1942, *Mrs. Miniver* explored the impact of war from its most personal angle, suggesting to Americans the need to fight for their most basic institutions. "The picture may be considered the final say on the superb and hellish struggle of English families from the beginning of the war until today," wrote John Mosher in *The New Yorker*. The film's concentration on a middle-class family's response to war (people "accustomed to nice things . . . with pleasant houses") attracted Americans who saw themselves in a similar light.[3]

Significantly, *Mrs. Miniver* did not minimize the changes—or losses—imposed by war, even though its major characters were somewhat "prissy and fake like all screen families."[4] Luftwaffe bombs rained from the sky, forcing the Minivers to spend long hours in their ill-equipped bomb shelter, and eventually confronting them with the partial destruction of their

"spacious, chintzy suburban home."[5] Furthermore, the Minivers were
not immune to war-caused deaths in their family or among their friends.
And Mr. Miniver was shown helping salvage the remains of the British
Expeditionary Force at Dunkirk, the military set-back considered most
devastating to the British.

While presenting the horrors of war with "persuasive wallop," *Mrs.
Miniver* also conveyed the gallantry uniquely possible for people under
great stress.[6] The Minivers faced the exigencies of war with courage and
determination, whether they were sending a son off to war or encountering a wounded German in the garden. And lower-class persons received
attention in *Mrs. Miniver* as well as middle- and upper-class people. The
cheerful stationmaster who grew roses was as important in the movie as
the aristocratic Lady Beldon, who patriotically surmounted her worries
about tradition and fading class distinctions in the course of the film.

The key figure in this movie that explained life on the home front
of America's most favored ally was, however, Kay Miniver. "Much of the
charm of the picture depends upon Greer Garson's Mrs. Miniver," *The
New Yorker*'s critic noted.[7] As the person in charge of a suburban
home and family, Mrs. Miniver's behavior revealed the public's expectations of women in her circumstances—women who were forced to confront the extraordinary caretaking duties imposed by an international crisis.
Since *Mrs. Miniver* vied with only one other film—*Yankee Doodle Dandy*
(Warner Brothers, 1942)—for top box-office honors in 1942, it appeared
that Americans were keenly interested in a plausible story of war's effect
on women's culture.

The action in the epic picture, *Mrs. Miniver*, begins during the summer
of 1939, a few months after Hitler's invasion of Poland thrusts the British
into World War II. Historians note that this period found "those in the
know—journalists, BBC officials, civil servants, and intelligent people
who read the foreign press . . . in a constant state of anxiety." But the
general public in England remained "blasé" or "optimistic," more involved with summer holidays than international events.[8] As the written
message at the beginning of *Mrs. Miniver* explains, "In 1939, the sun
shone down on a happy, careless people, who worked and played, reared
their children and tended their gardens in . . . happy, easy-going England."

The first episode of *Mrs. Miniver* gives viewers a picture of these
carefree days. The camera isolates Kay Miniver (Greer Garson) as she
hurries along London's crowded streets, mingling cheerfully with a busy,
rush-hour throng of people. Smartly dressed in an attractive suit and hat
(with the inevitable fur boa of the affluent woman draped over her shoul-

ders), arms laden with packages, Mrs. Miniver has obviously been on a pleasurable shopping trip into the city.

This chic lady's concerns in the months before the war are illustrated by her thoughts as she joins the line at the bus stop to begin her trip homeward. During the day, Kay Miniver has seen an irresistible hat—a stylish creation of fur and feathers—in a milliner's window, and despite the extravagance of such a purchase, she is reluctant to leave London without it. Although Mrs. Miniver manages to resist temptation long enough to board the bus, after a few blocks she springs to her feet, quickly leaves the bus, and rushes back to the milliner's, fretting all the way that someone else has stolen her prize. Relieved to find the hat still perched on display, Mrs. Miniver sighs to the salesclerk, "I don't know what my husband will say . . . But I've simply got to have it."

Comfortably seated in a first class compartment on the train home to Belham, Mrs. Miniver explains her purchase—and her general attitude—to a fellow passenger. A woman of England's middle class, she likes nice things, sometimes those far beyond her means, but especially, "pretty clothes, good schools for the children . . . the car and the garden." She is at times, she confides, upset at her own extravagance, but both she and her husband have "faith in their future."[9]

Mrs. Miniver's view and her small self-indulgence receive justification in the movie's next scene. Lady Beldon (Dame May Whitty), the local aristocrat of Belham, enters the compartment and starts a series of complaints about her day. A portly woman, resembling Queen Victoria draped in furs, Lady Beldon is obviously accustomed to special attention and a tyrant's role. She vigorously attacks the middle-class women who swarm about her favorite shops, insisting at the end of her tirade, "I don't know what the country is coming to. Everyone trying to be better than their betters." Mrs. Miniver's sweet, accepting smile, and her covert glance of approval at her own hat box, undoubtedly endeared her to American audiences of 1942, who disapproved of the British aristocracy as much as they shared Mrs. Miniver's middle-class values.[10]

The portraits of the two women strongly emphasize these attitudes. In contrast to Lady Beldon's snobbishness, Kay Miniver is a practicing egalitarian, friendly and gracious to everyone she encounters in her daily routine. At the end of her journey home, she pauses to chat with the local stationmaster, Mr. Ballard, whose hobby is cultivating exotic roses. The gentle, white-haired Mr. Ballard (Henry Travers) tells Mrs. Miniver of his latest accomplishment in horticulture, the creation of a rose of such perfection and beauty that he plans to defy tradition and enter it in the gentry's flower show, regardless of the objections of the formidable Lady Beldon, whose roses have always won first prize in the annual competition. Kay Miniver offers encouragement to Mr. Ballard and, in return, he asks if he might name his rose for the person whose personality it resembles—Mrs. Miniver.[11]

Fortified by this tribute, but still concerned about her architect-husband, Clem's (Walter Pidgeon) reaction to her new hat, Mrs. Miniver returns to her elegantly furnished home, a household of eight people, including the Minivers' three children, two servants, and a nursemaid. After a cheerful and affectionate reunion with her two younger children, Toby and Judy (Christopher Severn and Clare Sandars), and a more restrained greeting from son, Vin (Richard Ney), an Oxford student with a newly-discovered social consciousness, the Minivers enjoy a quiet dinner, nervously trying to decide how to break the news of mutual extravagance to each other.[12]

As the audience knows, Clem Miniver has also had a day of temptation—several pounds more expensive than an attractive hat. Mr. Miniver has purchased a new car, and after he blurts out this fact, he (and the audience) timorously await his wife's approval.

The accommodating Mrs. Miniver happily complies, supporting Clem's indulgence and casually remarking, when she later shows off her hat to Clem in their bedroom, that the furry headgear did not cost "too much for people with a car like ours."

To audiences in 1942, the opening scenes of *Mrs. Miniver* conveyed a sense of normal times in England, a period (according to the movie) when middle-class families concerned themselves with material acquisition and harmony with one another. The Minivers exemplified a financially comfortable, materially ambitious, happily married couple, devoted to their children and concerned with pleasing each other and sharing mutual goals. As the Minivers retire (into their twin beds) at the end of their day, Clem expresses his warm feelings to Kay: "I think you're even more beautiful than when I married you," he murmurs contentedly. And Kay responds, "I have more reason to be," while sending a last satisfied glance at her new hat.

Pre-war British society, while apparently idyllic for the Minivers, was also class-conscious and tradition-bound, as the movie admitted.[13] As the film continues its description of the days immediately preceding the Nazi invasion of Poland, the audience learns that the lower-class stationmaster's decision to enter his "Mrs. Miniver" rose in Lady Beldon's contest has created consternation among the defenders of the old ways. The *grande dame* of Belham is not particularly liked—while Mrs. Miniver is described (even by local gossips) as "the nicest lady in the neighborhood." Nevertheless, Kay Miniver is a newcomer, while Lady Beldon represents generations of noblesse oblige, and thus it would not be fitting for Mr. Ballard's "Mrs. Miniver" to win first prize in the competition.

The issue is sufficiently monumental in suburban Belham to bring the aristocracy into Kay Miniver's beautifully kept home. Lady Beldon's granddaughter, Carol, a confident, pretty brunette (Teresa Wright), comes calling to ask a personal favor. Pointing out that her grandmother is old, and that she has always taken great pride in her incomparable roses, Carol asks Kay Miniver to dissuade Mr. Ballard from competing in the flower show. Mrs. Miniver remains calm and poised during this scene, but her son, Vin, is furious with Carol Beldon for her selfish request, as opposed to her ideas as he is attracted by her lovely appearance. In a heated interchange, Vin insists that Carol is attempting to prolong the upper class' domination of the underprivileged—an "unconscionable action." Carol resists this view of her motives, accusing Vin of Oxford liberalism while remarking, "I've spent most of my holidays these past few years doing settlement work in the slums of luxury." Angry but chastened, Vin stalks from the room, but his objections have been noted. As a member of the younger generation of British aristocrats, Carol Beldon recognizes the need for change in England's rigid class structure. Smiling sweetly, she apologizes to Mrs. Miniver for overstepping her place, and withdraws her request.

Carol's receptivity to mixing with those below her station is further emphasized at the village dance, where her friendly and thoughtful behavior is more reminiscent of Kay Miniver than Lady Beldon. She even manages, on this festive night, to lure Vin out of his stormy mood, gently urging him to remember his sense of humor. Vin manages this feat, dropping his pomposity for the pleasures of dancing with Carol, who appears even more fetching in an evening gown.

Mrs. Miniver's depiction of pre-war happy, easy-going England ends with the convivial village dance, where the romantic feelings between a young man and woman supersede class distinctions. According to the film, the extant barriers to forming the British people into "a cooperating and mutually sympathetic unit" were rapidly disintegrating even before the war. The traditional authority of the upper class was being challenged and, in fact, an aggressive, consumer-oriented middle class formed the backbone of British society.

Thus the Minivers and their cohorts are the camera's targets when news of war comes. It is a Sunday, and the village has gathered to hear an eloquent sermon from the highly-respected Vicar (Henry Wilcoxon). He must offer instead the announcement of England's Declaration of War against Germany, which has just been broadcast.[14] The congregation, including the Minivers, calmly takes the news of war in stride, showing no surprise or panic and silently dispersing to prepare for their nation's defense.

The period that historians have labeled "the phony war" is shown as a troubled time for the Minivers, a time when Vin joins the Royal Air Force, Mr. Miniver volunteers for civilian defense duties, and a servant woman, Gladys (Brenda Forbes), loses her man, Horace (Rhys Williams) to the Army.[15] In contrast to the Minivers' stoic acceptance of their obligations, Gladys is fearful and emotional, openly crying over her loss and expressing some rebellion. Kay and Clem comfort Gladys, but they also counsel her to keep a stiff upper lip. She complies, camouflaging her concern behind formal dress (a chic hat, stylish coat, and gloves) when she must say good-bye to Horace, thus earning an oblique accolade from Clem: "Well, she's done you proud, Horace."

Just as war forces poise on an emotional Gladys, the pressures of imminent combat affect Carol Beldon's conservative attitudes toward romance. As Vin pursues her during his pilot training, her "I want to be sure" stance shifts to a "now or never" response. When Vin returns home on leave, shortly before Hitler's blitzkrieg of the Low Countries and France in the spring of 1940, he finds Carol a comfortable visitor to the Miniver household, and he is ecstatic when she cheerfully accepts his proposal of marriage during a family dinner.

The Minivers are very pleased with Vin's and Carol's decisions, but their shared, worried glances also illustrate the fears they have for this young couple's future. As soon as a toast is proposed for the engaged pair, Kay and Clem's fears are confirmed; the telephone rings, and Vin is recalled to his RAF base. While Vin packs his bag upstairs, Mrs. Miniver and Carol Beldon sit quietly together, instinctively comforting one another by huddling closer as they listen for footsteps descending the stairs. When Vin appears, they arise in unison and each embraces the departing pilot.

Vin's recall to active duty signals the beginning of the Nazi offensive and the end of the European "phony war." Soon Kay and Clem will themselves be involved in England's war against the fascists. An early morning call for Mr. Miniver's volunteer services on river patrol drags the two reluctantly out of bed, and while Kay Miniver dutifully makes sandwiches for her husband, she also worries about the effects of these long hours on his health. Nevertheless, she manages a bright smile and some caring words to Clem as he chugs off in his small boat.

And both will be needed, for Clem and countless other volunteers have been called to rescue the British Expeditionary Force at Dunkirk. In this "wonderfully exciting episode," a few small craft are first seen moving down the Thames, then others join in, and the visual impact of a growing "flotilla of amateur navigators" is complimented by a surging increase of sputtering motors on the soundtrack. On this quiet night, the swell of engines increases to a deafening roar, and small boats fill the mouth of the estuary before tackling the English Channel in a "mass scene . . . of great and thrilling heroism."[16]

Despite the obvious cinematographic pull of a rescue scene such as Dunkirk, *Mrs. Miniver* left the Englishmen in their fragile boats in the Channel, returning viewers to England and asking them to share Mrs. Miniver's "worrying."[17]

In this waiting scene, the audience learns that five days have passed since Clem's departure. Mrs. Miniver is shown pacing nervously in the garden, distracted from her conversation with Mr. Ballard by the sound of guns and her own preoccupation with the unknown whereabouts of her husband and son. Yet she is pleasant to the elderly stationmaster, maintaining a composed demeanor despite her anxiety. As Mr. Ballard leaves, and Kay resumes her restless morning walk, she is faced with a new, enormously frightening crisis. The feet and legs she spies beneath a bush turn out to belong—not to a mischievous English boy playing games—but to a wounded German pilot, as "fierce as a hunted animal."[18] Mrs. Miniver courageously tries to snatch the Nazi's gun, but desperation moves the pilot faster, and Kay Miniver is forced to prepare food and drink for the enemy in her immaculate English kitchen. During this encounter the German flier, a young man of Vin's age, is arrogant and demanding, full of praise for his fatherland and Hitler even on the verge of physical collapse. Mrs. Miniver's initial compassion for his injuries turns into determination as she listens to his "Aryan nonsense."[19] When the Nazi faints from weakness, Mrs. Miniver swiftly seizes his gun and calls the police. They arrive quickly, efficient and awed by Kay Miniver's resourcefulness. She, on the other hand, clings to her son, Toby, finally and personally aware of the caliber of England's Nazi enemy. Both Mrs. Miniver and the audience are now persuaded that the Germans' drive for power has placed them beyond the reach of human kindness or gracious actions.

Kay Miniver's grim realization is interrupted by the sound of a boat's engine which signals an exhausted Clem's return. As Kay joyfully performs her wifely duties, fussing over Clem, preparing food to assuage his hunger, and tucking him into bed, she hears the drone of airplane motors and rushing to the window, sees Vin's squadron returning to base. For brief moments Kay Miniver's world is once again intact.

The serious possibilities of war's intrusion into private domains is highlighted, however, in an ensuing dialogue between husband and wife.

Mr. Miniver playfully tells Kay after recounting the scene at Dunkirk, "I'm almost sorry for you—having such a nice, quiet, peaceful time when things were really happening. But that's what men are for, isn't it? To go out and do things while you womenfolk look after the house." Although Mrs. Miniver docilely replies, "Yes, dear," the audience is aware (as Clem will be soon) that women's duties in the home now include protecting it from an immediate and present enemy.

The German Air Force and the imminent Battle of Britain are not Mrs. Miniver's only problems, however. An equally formidable obstacle, Lady Beldon, comes to the Minivers' home to register her objections to Vin's and Carol's engagement, and Kay admits to her husband, "I am scared, just as I was when I took that German pilot." Nevertheless, Kay Miniver shows equal resourcefulness in her confrontation with the dowager, suggesting that in war "time is so precious to the young people." Lady Beldon recants, showing democratic leanings in her compliments to the Minivers, and Carol and Vin are married with both families' blessings, departing immediately for a honeymoon in Scotland.

The marriage between a woman of England's aristocracy and a man of the middle class seals the country's pledge to unity in *Mrs. Miniver*. As the Battle of Britain takes place, survival and death play no class favorites, and a commitment to the "People's War" is required of every English citizen.

As the first scene of total war occurs, the camera focuses on the Minivers, who flee to their shaky dugout in the backyard when the bombing starts. During this prolonged attack, Mrs. Miniver is the sustaining force in her family; her soft, melodious voice reading *Alice in Wonderland* presents a soothing contrast to the harsh sounds of exploding Luftwaffe bombs and anti-aircraft artillery. The Minivers' home is partially destroyed in this bombardment and the general community is severely damaged. But the first wave of Nazi aggression takes little toll in human life. The scene is haunting nonetheless: The small Minivers, Toby and Judy, cry out in their sleep, and Kay and Clem dwell on small, homey conversation—the cook's departure, Kay's knitting, the need for a new laundry service, tomorrow's flower show—to see themselves through the night's ordeal.

By the next day, the community of Belham considers itself veterans and, therefore, unlikely recipients of a second Luftwaffe visit. So the highly publicized flower show proceeds. Carol and Vin (just returned from their honeymoon) accompany Kay as she drives to the event. No sooner has this pleasant, calm gathering been sanctified by Lady Beldon's presentation of first prize to Mr. Ballard for his "Mrs. Miniver" rose, than air raid sirens intrude. As Vin dashes off to rejoin his squadron, Belham receives a second, devastating Luftwaffe attack.

Both Mr. Ballard and Carol are mortal victims of the return Nazi sweep, the kindly gardener dying within an hour of his proud acquisition of the Beldon Cup. Carol is fatally wounded as Kay Miniver drives their vulnerable car through the area of fighting, and in this scene, Mrs. Miniver is thoroughly tested. She and Carol begin their journey home in the dark, creeping along with no lights as bombs shriek and explode overhead. Stopping when they see a flaming plane come hurtling to the ground, Kay Miniver murmurs one desperate thought, "I want so much to get home," but this bastion is no longer impregnable. When she finally achieves her goal, it is with a seriously wounded daughter-in-law on her hands. Quelling her panic with effort, Mrs. Miniver comforts Carol in her soothing voice, "Don't be frightened . . . I'll get help." Carol gasps pleadingly, "You won't tell Vin," and Kay reassures her as she lovingly pulls a blanket over Carol and rushes to telephone for an ambulance. Returning with a glass of water in her hand, Mrs. Miniver finds her ministrations no longer necessary. Carol has died, and Kay must again face the cruelties of war within her home. Rocking Carol's body, her face twisted in anguish, Mrs. Miniver sobs into the dead girl's hair, "God, oh God."

The movie leaves the Minivers trying to cope with the inevitable losses demanded by war. In the last scene, the Miniver family is once again at church, a bombed shell of its former medieval glory. Lady Beldon sits by herself, a lonely figure decrying war's cost. The wise Vicar sums up the meaning of this war for the beleaguered British: "This is not only a war of soldiers in uniform, it is a war of the people—of all the people—and it must be fought, not only on the battlefield, but in the cities and the villages, in the factories and on the farms, in the home and in the heart of every man, woman and child who loves freedom!"

And in *Mrs. Miniver*'s ending scene, the survivors of "the tyranny and terror that threaten to strike us down," offer support and comfort to one another. Vin switches pews, joining the forlorn Lady Beldon, and as the choir sings "Onward Christian Soldiers," the unified congregation gazes upward, sending their prayers to the RAF planes that swoop to the defense of Britain.

Americans showed a strong interest in films about their British ally in 1942. The English had, after all, survived the Nazi's ravage of their cities and countrysides, and during a year of troubled losses in the Pacific, Americans found succor in an ally's successful resistance.[20] According to box-office receipts, *Mrs. Miniver* was the most popular of the movies exploring the courageous defiance of the British. But *Eagle Squadron* (Walter Wanger Studios, released through Universal), a story of volunteer flyers from the United States in the RAF, and *This Above All* (20th Century-Fox), a poignant tale of a lower-class British deserter who overcomes his bitterness against the English upper class and returns to fight for his country, also attracted large audiences.[21]

Other war films received similar public support in 1942. *To The Shores of Tripoli* (20th Century-Fox) focused on the difficult but heroic pace required of men in the United States Marine Corps, while *Captains of the Clouds* (Warner Brothers) stressed cooperation among Canadian pilots. James Cagney's portrayal of George M. Cohan in *Yankee Doodle Dandy* (WB) earned unqualified praise from reviewers and the grand, patriotic, musical scenes in the film offered notable inspiration for people gearing themselves to a major war effort.[22]

Mrs. Miniver touched the American psyche in special ways, however. While few citizens of the United States would undergo the rigorous training of the Marine Corps or fly planes in combat, many were convinced in 1942 that they might encounter a German or Japanese saboteur in their backyards.[23] And Americans were also aware that war meant a disruption of their personal ambitions, whether that entailed purchasing a new car or hat—or simply living an uninterrupted, peaceful life.

In this sense, *Mrs. Miniver* captured the current concerns of Americans, a people newly arrived to the theater of war and anxious for guidance. The movie did not disappoint its fans; it neatly synthesized the strengths that Americans brought to their new ordeal, camouflaging them beneath a veneer of a nation already three years at war. Suburban Belham reflected more of American society than its British counterpart, regardless of the trappings of British aristocracy and middle-class persons indulged by servants.[24] And Kay Miniver's characteristics and actions were distinctly in the tradition of the American folklore that defined woman's place.

Kay Miniver's portrait, in fact, struck a nice balance between the rural and urban heroines who vied for domination in American popular thought before the outbreak of World War II. She was a middle-class, suburban woman, happily and competently playing a traditional role, but at the same time, Mrs. Miniver was enormously resourceful when faced with crises. Her characterization includes both the attributes of the old ways of Mother York and Gracie in *Sergeant York* and the dynamism and intelligence of Ann Mitchell in *Meet John Doe*. In *Mrs. Miniver*, the fusion of old and new ways was apparent.

In the months before England's involvement in war, Kay Miniver's concerns were shown to be those of the typical American housewife whose husband earned enough money to enable her to have some help around the house.[25] Free from the constant demands of cooking, house-cleaning and watching over her small children, Mrs. Miniver devoted her time to community affairs and the pursuit of nice things. Although worried about her tendencies to extravagance, Kay obviously enjoyed being a consumer, and one suspects (after watching the first segment of the movie) that she had a lengthy history of getting her way in such matters. Her plaintive sigh to the salesclerk, "I don't know what my husband will say, but I've got to have it," conveyed the impression that, in her eagerness to own pretty clothes, Mrs. Miniver's desire to please herself superseded her husband's authority, even though he was the sole breadwinner in the family.

Of course, maintaining harmony in her family was also a duty that Kay Miniver took seriously. Therefore she waited for the proper moment to tell Clem of her purchase. While Mr. Miniver chose a public forum, the dinner table, to reveal his acquisition of a new car, Kay selected the privacy of their bedroom, when she was clad alluringly in a silk night-gown, to bring up the topic of her hat. Clem's repeated references to his wife as a beautiful woman in this intimate scene drew an obvious link. Mrs. Miniver's strengths in the money game were her attractiveness and sexuality, and both appeared to serve her well.

The sexual motif aseptically presented in *Mrs. Miniver* was a common one in movies of the 1930s, when the harsh depression years left women with "nothing to sell but sex."[26] This attitude had been moderated by 1941 as both *Sergeant York* and *Meet John Doe* illustrated. While Gracie and Ann Mitchell rewarded their romantic interests with kisses and embraces, it was for their men's proper behavior and idealism.[27] In *Mrs. Miniver*, on the other hand, Kay's sexual favors were associated with gaining her husband's approval for the purchase of luxury, consumer items. In the bedroom scene, Kay was both manipulative—sweetly underscoring her husband's extravagance when showing off her hat—and a submissive, accommodating person, ostensibly accepting Clem's view of household finances and her own worth as a person: "You're really quite a beautiful woman, aren't you?" Clem complimented. "If you say so, darling," Kay replied (while casting a triumphant look at her hat).

Mrs. Miniver, then, suggested that the characteristics of an American suburban housewife included a propensity to spend money and a capacity for manipulating husbands into an accepting frame of mind. Where rural heroines were much more cautious, leaving financial matters in their men's hands, and urban heroines took charge of their own live-lihoods, the suburban heroine did a bit of both. Mrs. Miniver defined herself partly as a consumer and spent accordingly, but she also required her husband's approval, and she gained it by agreeably boosting his ego in public and private.

The movie invited no criticisms of Mrs. Miniver's characteristics or behavior in pre-war time. In fact, the Miniver family was shown to be charming and gracious, the epitome of the American success story. The worth of the Minivers' middle-class style of life, consumer problems included, was emphasized by the aristocratic Lady Beldon's pretentiousness and by the town's general consensus that Mrs. Miniver was the nicest lady in the neighborhood, who deserved a rose in her name if not the nobility's first prize.

When war came, the Minivers of Belham swiftly adjusted to the new circumstances. As loyal citizens, they rallied both to civilian defense and military duty. Moreover, their confidence in themselves and their country was shown to inspire both lower-class persons such as Gladys and Horace and the redoubtable Lady Beldon, who conceded to Kay that persons of the Minivers' ilk formed the "backbone of the society." The aristocrat's admission came during a personal conversation with Mrs. Miniver, and it was Belham's nicest lady who received the thrust of the compliments. In contrast to *Sergeant York* and *Meet John Doe*, the 1942 best-selling film cast a woman into the limelight, making her a spokesperson and delineating women's strengths—and obligations—when war threatened their domain.

Thus the film's allegiance to Kay Miniver's trials during wartime revealed both the importance of the suburban housewife in American folklore and the behavior expected of her. A consumer as well as a family harmonizer, Mrs. Miniver had to shift her priorities during the siege of Britain, ignoring the acquisition or preservation of material goods, and concentrating all her energies on her family's welfare and her national defense.[28]

Kay Miniver managed this switch without developing a gray hair. When Nazis destroyed the nice things that she had accumulated through the years, she spoke gratefully of the family's survival. And she performed the role of nurturer with gracious finesse. In spite of her worries, Kay exuded confidence to Clem when he left on his mysterious mission in the early morning, and she presented the same enthusiastic countenance to Vin when he was called to the nation's defense. Moreover, Mrs. Miniver easily calmed her family during the frightening episode in the bomb shelter, projecting the image of a woman who constantly thought of others before herself.

Like Mother York, Kay Miniver was shown to draw courage from religious beliefs in troubled times; however, the church was not her only source of strength. Unlike the rural women depicted in *Sergeant York*,

Mrs. Miniver grasped the issues involved in the war against the fascists. This knowledge was important in providing her with the resources for handling the "Aryan nonsense" she heard spouting from the German pilot's lips. When the Nazi invaded her domain, Mrs. Miniver was alert and ingenious, offering compassion but not allowing her concern or fear to dull her wit. Her actions in this and other scenes of war emergencies closely paralleled the venturesome qualities of Ann Mitchell—but in Kay Miniver's case, the audience knew that she was not seduced by false gods; indeed, this middle-class woman had both patriotism and righteousness on her side.

In blending the ways of the traditional and new woman, *Mrs. Miniver* gave credit to both. Kay Miniver was equally a capable nurturer and an enviable adventurer. Whether she was managing her traditional domains (negotiating with her husband, disciplining the children, convincing Lady Beldon of the value of romantic love in marriage, furthering closeness among people by supporting Mr. Ballard's challenge to the gentry) or whether she was entering male spheres (confronting the enemy in the garden, encountering Nazi bullets while driving home), Mrs. Miniver was endlessly resourceful. Her portrait offered reassurance to Americans that women could sustain their traditional institutions while meeting the crises generated by war.

Flexibility and a willingness to change were shown to be important characteristics in this effort. By the end of the movie, Mrs. Miniver "has learned quite a new way of living," shedding her pre-war concerns with ease and bearing up remarkably when bereft of male support.[29] Her major aid and comfort, in fact, came from other women. Lady Beldon offered Kay Miniver continual praise—culminating in her reluctant capitulation at the flower show because of Mrs. Miniver's gaze. "You have such a way of looking at people!" the dowager exclaimed as she too showed an ability to change.

Carol Beldon was shown to be a flexible and open person even before the war. But the Nazi assault "spans age and disarms traditional rivalries," forging a close, loving relationship between Carol and her mother-in-law.[30] In several scenes in the movie Mrs. Miniver and Carol shared their secret fears with one another, discussing the possibility of Vin's death and the terrors of war. This women's talk was reserved for their private moments, and they swiftly assumed cheerful faces whenever men appeared. The tragedy of Carol's death, however, was intensified by the closeness between these two women; Mrs. Miniver lost her major confidante as well as a new member of the family in the grim and touching death scene.

By 1942, the Bureau of Motion Pictures in the Office of War Information had published guidelines for the Hollywood industry, suggesting ways in which films could "show women what they can do in their homes to promote the war effort." The manual included this dictum: "It is part of the job of motion pictures to make the issues of the war clear and concrete realities to the millions of American women in order that they will be militant spokesmen for democracy, economic and religious freedom, racial equality and for all the other things that make America worth fighting for." By focusing on women's domains, *Mrs. Miniver* eloquently conveyed the message that all free women must join in the fight. More importantly, the portrait of Kay Miniver illustrated the resources the typical American housewife brought to the task, at least in the folklore of the nation. By fusing the traditions of the old and new images of women, *Mrs. Miniver* offered Americans a formula for war out of their own past.[31]

Like the epic story that ran before it, the finale of the movie confirmed society's need for the contributions of "Mrs. Minivers." The RAF planes viewed through the bombed ceiling of the cathedral in Belham were no more important to the nation's defense than the stalwart persons who quietly prayed in the remnants of their church. The lasting impression of the film echoed the Bureau of Motion Pictures' pronouncement: "without the home life which [the housewife] makes and preserves, we would have no strong, united nation."[32]

Of course, Mrs. Miniver's home and family—although sorely threatened—were still somewhat intact at the movie's conclusion. As the war progressed and filmmakers attempted to record its impact, the camera moved into Nazi-dominated countries where Hollywood's fictional women were fugitives or characters who faced the destruction of the power base within their traditional domains—women menaced with an ideology that wished to drive them back "to their medieval status in society."[33]

Women Behind Enemy Lines

While few war films reached top box-office status in 1941 or 1942, the second full year of war found Americans eager to purchase tickets to Hollywood's versions of World War II.[1] The best-selling movies of 1943 reflected Americans' interests in inspirational, flag-waving features, movies that visualized the combat front, and films that probed the nature of the enemy. Musical extravaganzas such as *This Is the Army* (WB), *Stage Door Canteen* (United Artists), *Thousands Cheer* (MGM), *Thank Your Lucky Stars* (WB), and *Star Spangled Rhythm* (Paramount), followed the example of *Yankee Doodle Dandy* (WB, 1942) in stirring patriotic fervor through songs and dance numbers. Millions of Americans relived the startling news of Pearl Harbor and the first, disastrous months of war in the Pacific with the crew of the "Mary Jane" in *Air Force* (WB), while Americans cheered the bombing of Japanese soil depicted in *Destination Tokyo* (WB). Other combat films followed troops into the harsh, African desert (*Immortal Sergeant*, 20th Century-Fox) and onto the high seas, where Nazi destroyers and submarines proved believable enemies (*In Which We Serve*, United Artists). The Japanese were shown to be equally committed adversaries in the Pacific in both Paramount's story of Army nurses, *So Proudly We Hail*, and in 20th Century-Fox's account of Marines forcing beachheads in *Guadalcanal Diary*.

Foremost among the box-office hits of 1943 were three films that explored the nature of totalitarian societies and the threat which their militaristic structures posed to the American way of life.[2] Two of these popular movies—*Hitler's Children* and *Behind the Rising Sun*—were "B" grade, low budget films, adapted from written eyewitness accounts by RKO screenwriter, Emmet Lavery, and director, Edward Dmytryk.[3] In spite of the "jumbled ideology" of both films, they struck a responsive chord among Americans, who flocked to theaters to see the Nazi and Japanese "indoctrination machines" in action.[4] The third film which explored the effects of fascist control was *Casablanca* (WB), a spy thriller set in French Morocco. This enormously popular movie featured Nazis as cultured swine, as adept at ordering caviar and champagne as they were at eliminating or torturing members of the Underground.[5]

Each of these films dealt with displaced people—characters who were fugitives from the Nazis, or anti-fascists who had become aliens within their own societies. *Casablanca*, whose locale was a fringe area of Nazi-dominated Europe, cast both men and women in the roles of resisters to fascism (with an accent on the former). But as Hollywood's cameras sought to capture the extreme regimentation within the Third Reich and Imperial Japan, women characters were hoisted into prominent display. In both *Hitler's Children* and *Behind the Rising Sun*, the male leads, although exposed to American culture in their formative years, yielded to fascist propaganda and became military participants in their countries' armies in their adult years. On the other hand, Anna Muller and Tama, heroines similarly touched by American influence, consistently resisted the ideas of the fascists, even under threat of torture and death. Since these heroines' strengths appear to derive from their commitment to American ideals (Anna was a United States citizen, Tama a secretary to an American entrepreneur), their opposition to fascism reminded movie-goers of women's importance as moral guardians, while also emphasizing that women in the United States were "inheritors of a tradition of courage, independence and achievement."[6]

The three films also delineated the institutions and values considered most important to American women in the mid-war years. The heroines in *Casablanca, Hitler's Children*, and *Behind the Rising Sun* were cast adrift from their traditional moorings. They were rejected by the men they loved; they were compelled to give up their dreams of pleasant, secure homes; and they had to cope with a continual life of flight, or the terrors of forced prostitution, or the reality of Nazi sterilization laboratories. As the women's lives unfolded in the three dramas, a picture emerged of fascism's most dire threat to the American way of life, and the institutions most challenged were those within women's traditional culture: romantic love, an unfettered choice of mate, the freedom to have children when wife and husband willed, the sanctity of marriage and family, the privacy of the home, and the ability to experience uninterrupted time in which to strengthen a relationship.

Ilsa, the fugitive heroine in *Casablanca*, illustrated the plight of the homeless woman most poignantly. She was a thoroughly displaced person, unwelcome in her Nazi-occupied country, bereft of the security of women's traditional domains, and without a job that offered her a sense of identification. Shorn of these symbols of protection, Ilsa was easily interpreted as a woman who "is simply there—beautiful, soft, remote, warm, mysterious, the impossible object of an impossible romance, the dream lover of every man."[7]

There was more substance in Ilsa's characterization, however, than this paean admits, as an analysis of *Casablanca* shows.

Casablanca (Warner Brothers, 1943)

Completed late in 1942, Warner Brothers' *Casablanca* thrilled audiences of its immediate era and lived to become a classic.[8] Although the smoldering romance between Richard Blaine (Humphrey Bogart) and Ilsa Lund (Ingrid Bergman) dominates many film-goers' memories of the top-grossing movie, director Michael Curtiz's *Casablanca* was very much a war film which educated the American public to the fact of a Nazi-controlled Europe and dramatized the agonies of refugees who sought to escape the Third Reich. Commenting on the picture in an evaluation written for the Library of Congress and the Intelligence Division of the Office of War Information, analyst Philip T. Hartung noted that "*Casablanca* is a melodrama in which all the characters are in some way connected with the war . . . In the finale . . . our side [the United Nations] triumphs."[9]

Casablanca opens with a frequently used instructional device of the war years. An unseen narrator with a typical newsreel voice informs the audience that "with the coming of the Second World War, many eyes in imprisoned Europe turned hopefully or desperately toward the freedom of the Americas." While the camera focuses on a map of Europe and Northern Africa, the lesson continues:

> Lisbon became the great embarkation point. But not everyone could get to Lisbon directly. And so a tortuous, roundabout refugee trail sprang up. Paris to Marseilles . . . Across the Mediterranean to Oran. Then by train or auto or foot across the rim of Africa to Casablanca in French Morocco. Here the fortunate ones through money or influence or luck, might obtain exit visas and scurry to Lisbon. And from Lisbon to the new world. But the others wait in Casablanca and wait and wait and wait.

With the importance of Casablanca established, the camera moves into the Café Americain, a nightclub owned by the mysterious and aloof Rick Blaine. The café is the center of entertainment and intrigue in the teeming city, providing a haven for adventurers as well as refugees. The inscrutable Rick presides over the elegant casino and bar with a manner befitting a monarch. He is carefully neutral in politics (a posture used to convey this displaced American's deep cynicism in the time frame of the film—early December, 1941), and wields considerable personal power, summarily ousting obstreperous drunks (including a woman who professes love for him) and denying gambling privileges to a prosperous German banker who displeases him. Moreover, Rick commands an imperial loyalty from his staff, including waiters, bartenders, and most of all Sam, a black piano-player and singer, who has been with Rick for years.[10] Rick's royal air is further conveyed by his custom of not drinking with his clientele. Although the head of the black market in Casablanca, Ferrari (Sidney Greenstreet), suggests to Rick early in the film that "isolationism is no longer a practical policy," Blaine insists that he will "stick my neck out for nobody," a stance applauded as a "wise foreign policy" by Captain Louis Renault, the French Prefect of Police in Unoccupied French Morocco (Claude Rains). By placing himself above human involvement, Rick can enjoy an affluent lifestyle, bribing the amiable Renault for favors and freely trading insults with the arrogant representative of the Third Reich, Major Heinrich Strasser (Conrad Veidt). When asked his nationality by the latter, Blaine replies, "I'm a drunkard." And when pressed for his political loyalties, Rick smoothly sidesteps: "Your business is politics," he tells Strasser, "Mine is running a saloon."

The reasons for Rick's coldness and apolitical stance are rooted deep in his past, a part of which is revealed as the film progresses. In more sentimental days, Rick espoused causes, running guns to Italy's target, Ethiopia, in 1935, and fighting for the Loyalists during the Spanish Civil War. In 1940 he fled Paris barely in front of the German victors, defiantly drinking champagne with his friend, Henri, as the Germans marched into the city. Such streaks of youthful idealism are submerged in the present Rick, and the audience finds that his determination to "stick his neck out for nobody" was born—not as the result of political defeat—but because of a failure in personal life. Rick is soured because he has lost in love.

The action that reveals Rick's source of disillusionment begins in the busy Café Americain on a usual evening. A desperate black market runner, Ugarte (Peter Lorre), who had earlier extracted from an unwilling Rick his promise to safeguard two stolen letters of transit, enters the nightclub. The documents are of extreme importance, for Casablanca contains many refugees who would pay highly for such secure passage to America. Ugarte hopes to sell them for a huge profit, but instead this theft will cost him his life. Major Strasser has flown into the city to insure the punishment of the guilty Ugarte, and in a display calculated to impress the German major, Captain Renault's gendarmes descend on Ugarte at the café and capture him when he attempts to escape. Ugarte is later eliminated, but the letters of transit are safe in Sam's piano. Rick's possession of these important exit visas now catapults him into the tangle of politics, prey to the suspicions of Major Strasser, and the possible savior of the fleeing Czech leader of the European Underground, Victor Laszlo (Paul Henreid) and the woman with whom he is traveling, Ilsa Lund.

The uproar over Ugarte's capture is no sooner quieted than this couple, newly arrived to Casablanca, enter the Café Americain. A ripple of interest follows them to their table, for they are a striking pair and Laszlo's fame has preceded them. True to his penchant for pretty faces and shrewd politics, the suave Renault quickly pays homage, particularly to Ilsa: "I was informed that you were the most beautiful woman ever to visit Casablanca. That was a gross understatement."[11] Seemingly accustomed to such compliments, Ilsa murmurs an unaffected "You are so kind," and turns her attention to Sam, whose piano is located fortuitously next to their table. Greeting Sam warmly as an old friend, Ilsa persuades him to play an old favorite, "As Time Goes By." Sam's reluctance to please this lady is understood swiftly as the camera follows Rick's reaction to the first strains of the song. Electrified and angry, he storms toward Sam, beginning savagely, "I told you never to play that song . . ." and halts abruptly as his eyes light on Ilsa. Although Rick and Ilsa remain formal and composed during the introductions and following conversation, powerful undercurrents are obvious to the audience. Ilsa's face glows luminously as she gazes at Rick and he performs two unprecedented actions: he drinks with his customers and he insists on paying for the champagne. After closing time, Rick continues to drink and his reminiscences take us to the Paris of 1940 in the days before German occupation when he and Ilsa were in love and confidently planning a future together.

Seen through Rick's memory, the days in Paris are idyllic indeed. Ilsa is a devoted companion, intelligent, spunky, and full of laughter. The two have carved a personal world of caring for each other even in a war-torn country on the verge of collapse. They determine to leave Paris only because Ilsa fears for Rick's fate if he is captured by the Germans.[12] Yet Ilsa does not appear on the afternoon of their scheduled departure by train. Rick paces the overcrowded railway station, his coat and hat limited protection against the torrential rain, and finds that at the last moment Ilsa sends only a note, pleading with him to go without her for they must not see each other again. As the rain washes the words from Ilsa's letter, Rick climbs on the train, a defeated and embittered man.

As Rick returns to the present from this time gone by, Ilsa appears in the dark and empty nightclub. With brimming eyes, she attempts to tell him the reason for her abandonment of him in Paris, starting with her experiences as a young girl when she met "a very great and courageous man . . . who opened up for her a whole beautiful world, full of knowledge and thoughts and ideals." Everything she knew or ever became was because of this great man, she mistily recalls, and "she looked up to him, worshipped him." Ilsa gets no further with this story of her life. Drunk and hurt, Rick sneers at this sentimental account, preferring to see Ilsa as simply an unfaithful woman, accustomed to using and discarding men on her own terms. "Who was it you left me for?" he demands. "Was it Laszlo—or were there others in between? Or aren't you the kind that tells?" Insulted, Ilsa leaves, and grief once again engulfs Rick, who slumps tiredly on the table.

The tone of the next film sequence lifts viewers from the gloom of broken promises and estranged lovers into the sun-drenched bazaars of a refugee-flooded city. Apparently immune to hangovers, Rick is once again his debonair, resourceful self as he seeks out the chief of the city's black market, Ferrari, to discuss Ugarte's fate and the "missing" letters of transit. Rick also encounters Ilsa in the open marketplace, fingering lace in a desultory manner. Although Rick hastens to apologize for his prior hostile conduct, Ilsa is aloof and unforgiving, waiting until the moment she sweeps away from Blaine to disclose the reason for her desertion in Paris and her current loyalty to Laszlo: "Victor Laszlo is my husband," she informs Rick. Stunned by this news, Rick returns to his café to brood. Meanwhile, Ferrari shows hidden loyalties to the Allies by divulging Blaine's possession of the letters of transit to the Laszlos. Rick, formerly fastidiously neutral in politics, is now placed squarely in an unsought moral dilemma as the film poses the question: Will Blaine abide by the rules of Vichy France and Nazi Germany and his own self-interest, or will he overcome his personal cynicism and aid the Allied cause, symbolized by the leader of the European Underground?

The eventual answer to this question is foreshadowed in two sequences, although opposing scenes occur to maintain the tension of the film. Rick's generous, caring nature is revealed when he accompanies a woman, who has been forced into a sexual agreement with Renault in exchange for visas for herself and her husband, to the Café Americain's crooked roulette table. Rick's casual nod to the croupier allows the woman's husband to win sufficient money to buy the exit papers, prompting Renault to accuse Rick (with some pique) of being a "sentimentalist." And, in one of the more dramatically moving moments of the film, Rick illustrates his hidden loyalty to the Allied cause when he permits his band of musicians to follow Laszlo's leadership; in the ensuing scene Nazi officers singing

mined reluctance from isolation to commitment. Blaine did not occupy center stage alone, however. The character of Ilsa Lund (portrayed by the extremely capable and highly photogenic Ingrid Bergman) was also important, showing in its development, the extant folklore about displaced women in the world at war.

According to Ilsa's role, such women lived exciting, turbulent, daring lives, but they were also enormously vulnerable. Only unusual women—those possessing exceptional beauty and rare loyalty and courage—could survive displacement from their countries and their traditional domains, and even these unique persons encountered severe problems. Without uncommon qualities, women adrift in a male-dominated society at war became barflies and prostitutes, selling their allegiances to the Allied cause as well as their bodies.

Ilsa was, of course, one of the unusual women, whereas the only other female character in *Casablanca* to receive any screen time, a displaced Frenchwoman, Yvonne, turned to drink when Rick rejected her and afterward appeared in the Café Americain on the arm of a German officer. While Yvonne "shows her true colors and patriotism later . . . [singing] with the group who is shouting "La Marseillaise," Ilsa's loyalties to the United Nations were never in doubt.[15] Her weaknesses lay in a more subtle choice—whether the cause of freedom and the sanctity of the marriage contract would overcome her desires to escape the maelstrom entirely, grabbing her chance for the normal life with her romantic love.

Despite Ilsa's uncommon qualities, she was still a woman who was primarily concerned with human relationships and her own part in them. Like Mrs. Miniver, she had an intellectual comprehension of war issues, shown both in her confrontation with Major Strasser and in her angry accusation to Rick in his apartment: "There's so much at stake and all you can think of is your own feeling." But Ilsa's complexities mainly lay in the emotional realm, and in this movie peopled by stoic and cynical men, she served to alert the audience to the world beyond talk and violent action—the inner world of human relationships, where feelings of pain, fear, caring, and doubt had precedence.

Thus Ilsa's face was a constant barometer of the amount of danger Laszlo was courting at any given time and it was through her expressions that viewers learned of the cost of being a fugitive in the Underground. Similarly, the currents that flowed between Rick and Ilsa were most obvious in her manner and gestures (although Bogart's tough guy image was considerably softened in this role). Ilsa's own personal pain was quite apparent also; as Sam acceded to her desire to hear "As Time Goes By" the camera dwelt on Ilsa's face, acquainting the audience with a deeply-felt tragedy somewhere in her past which she nevertheless had managed to survive with dignity.

Poise and dignity were, in fact, Ilsa's major coping strategies in this world at war. Like her beauty and loyalty, they were shown to be unusual qualities that set her apart from other displaced women. The film carefully built Ilsa's image of mystery and uniqueness, beginning with womanizer Renault's florid compliment when viewers were treated to their first studied camera shot of Ilsa. And Ilsa's rare loyalty was affirmed by various references in the movie explaining that she had steadfastly refused to leave Laszlo in spite of considerable danger to herself. Ilsa's poise and dignity enabled her to remain friendly and confident in the hostile, threatening milieu of nightclubs and constant intrigue.

Yet, despite Ilsa's arsenal of unusual qualities, her life as a fugitive—alienated from her country, her traditional work, women friends, and a publicly acknowledged marriage—wore her down. By the time she reached Casablanca, her fearful, nomadic existence with Victor had taken its toll, and she was a vulnerable woman, eager to escape her nightmarish life. When Rick and Ilsa met again in the Café Americain, her commitment to her husband and his work in the Underground was sorely challenged.

For the love story in *Casablanca* did not follow the usual girl-meets-boy Hollywood formula. In fact, the existence of the love-triangle created an immediate impression that at least one person would be required to sacrifice a relationship of importance to him or her. In time of war, the film suggested, relationships were as shifty and unpredictable as the state of world politics, and conventional institutions such as marriage were as severely questioned as traditional foreign policy.

The ambiguity surrounding Ilsa's associations with Victor and Rick served as a testimonial to this situation. Viewers did not learn, for example, that Ilsa and Victor Laszlo were married until Ilsa's involvement with both men had been well established. When Victor and Ilsa first appeared in the Café Americain (the night Ugarte was captured), they related to one another with affection and consideration, epitomizing a loyal, caring couple. However, in Rick's drunken flashback to Paris, Ilsa was shown expressing those same qualities with Rick, plus a tremendous, heady attachment. The two were constantly close in physical terms—embracing, standing next to each other, rubbing arms, and one could easily speculate from the hotel scene, sleeping together. Although Rick (when drunk) accused Ilsa of being a loose woman with an easy allegiance to men, the audience was not persuaded. Even before the actual circumstances of Ilsa's affair with Rick were described, her demeanor had suggested a chaste and selective woman. She was a woman whom men wished to marry—even the enigmatic Rick. He in fact broached the idea to her as they planned to leave Paris before the Germans arrived. In this last Parisian encounter, the viewers were much more aware than Rick that something was wrong; that Ilsa was struggling with a moral dilemma that required her to say good-bye to Rick. "Kiss me as if it was the last time," she pleaded, and Rick laughingly complied. The exact nature of this forced separation was not disclosed until the final scene between Ilsa and Rick. Only then did the audience discover that Ilsa had been obligated to keep her marriage to Victor a secret, for fear of reprisals from the fascists, and that she had thought him dead during her interval with Rick in Paris. War, the film explained, created new and unusual situations: husbands missing in action, women bereft of male support in strange cities, bittersweet love affairs "with the whole world crumbling." Displaced women had to develop strategies for handling the violation of their particular domains—marriage, the home, the family—just as men had to risk their lives in combat or Underground resistance to the enemy. In her first moment of temptation, Ilsa responded with classic fidelity, sacrificing her love for Rick, and preserving the illusion of her virtue by protecting each man from knowledge of the other. Even in her moments of closest intimacy with Rick, Ilsa maintained her loyalty to Laszlo, continually parrying Rick's curiosity about her former life with a smiling warning: "We promised no questions." And she did not share the news of Laszlo's escape from a Nazi concentration camp with Rick, preferring to vanish mysteriously from his life rather than risk an open confrontation. Although she was the victim of the exigencies of war as much as either man, Ilsa's role was to honor her commitment to her husband and her wedding vows, and she acceded to these expectations in Paris, smothering her private pain and dedicating herself to Victor and his cause.

By the time of Ilsa's second temptation in Casablanca, however, she was a more fragile woman, exhausted by the relentless pursuit of the Nazis, and in her desperation, near a breaking point. Although she admired Victor and wanted to believe in his work, it was her appreciation of duty that provided her sustenance for this role; she did not love Laszlo in the same mystical, passionate sense that drew her to Rick.[16] In the beautifully enacted confrontation scene, when Blaine invited Ilsa to "go ahead and shoot me," she was at the end of her resources and dissolved into tears. The sympathy of the audience was with Ilsa at this moment, suggesting that social mores in the America of the early 1940s clearly permitted—and perhaps encouraged—such overt moments of anguish and indecision in women. Emotional scenes forged a bond between unusual and ordinary women, illustrating their shared traits and common culture.

Responding to Ilsa's sorrow, the cynical Rick could finally show his dormant compassion and love—and as he provided support for her, Ilsa could also be weak and vulnerable without shame; together they understood and gave support to the submerged aspects of themselves. As the denouement of the film illustrates, however, this was not a feasible wartime combination. Succumbing to personal priorities, Ilsa went too far in her moment of capitulation. Eager to escape her confining liaison with Victor, she attempted to deny her ability to make life decisions for herself, exclaiming to Rick: "You have to think for both of us . . . for all of us."

Such abrogation of duty was not permitted even to displaced women in time of war. By the actions of her honorable lover, Ilsa was once again placed in her proper wifely role, and enormous credit was given to that position: "Inside of us we both know you belong with Victor," Rick explained to Ilsa at the airport. "You're part of his work, the thing that keeps him going." And lest Ilsa grow restive with her supportive role, Rick continued, "I'm no good at being noble, but it doesn't take much to see that the problems of three little people don't amount to a hill o' beans in this crazy world. Some day you'll understand this."

Of course, the lasting impression from the film's ending was that homeless, displaced Ilsa understood personal sacrifice all too well. Once again relying on poise and dignity, she murmured feelingly to Rick, "God bless you," and boarded the Lisbon-bound plane with her husband. In *Casablanca*, the marriage commitment, central to American life in the 1940s, triumphed. Once again a durable institution had withstood the onslaught of fascist treachery, the film implied. When romantic love and duty clashed, there could be no genuine doubt as to the choice that American women (and men) needed to make.

Hitler's Children (RKO, 1943)

Fugitive heroines such as Ilsa Lund Laszlo existed in a volatile world— a glamorous and exciting circle where anti-fascists' valor and honor were tested, but no important persons died (except the enemy). The controlled society of the Third Reich offered less flexibility, even to the most courageous persons. *Hitler's Children*, a film adapted from Gregor Ziemer's eyewitness account, *Education for Death*, detailed the coercive nature of Adolph Hitler's empire, presenting "aspects of the Nazi system and culture which had not been seen before on the screen."[17]

Although a low-budget movie, *Hitler's Children* received praise from analysts in the Bureau of Intelligence of the Office of War Information as well as attracting an exceptional number of movie-goers. In January of 1942 BOI writers evaluating Hollywood productions explained that "representations of the nature of our enemies continued as they have in the past. No picture presented a revealing or realistic portrayal of what our enemies are like or of their motives."[18] The February report of these same officials was more optimistic. "One film . . . did point up the character of the Nazi regime," they recorded. "*Hitler's Children* was the first extended treatment of the Nazis issued since these studios began."[19]

The same analysts conceded that the movie had weaknesses: "The film will not enlighten the American public as to the source of Nazi power over the Germans," a weekly summary of movies insisted; however, the film did attempt to elucidate the horrifying restrictions which the Nazis had placed upon all persons under their control.[20]

Significantly, the limitations imposed by the Nazis' militaristic, dictatorial system were shown to damage women's conventional domains more harshly than other institutions in society. American-born Anna Muller, the rebel heroine in *Hitler's Children*, struggled against the totalitarian destruction of "the traditionally sacred elements of society: i.e., marriage, the home, and the church, not to mention love."[21] Men joined her in this effort, acceding to the popular folklore that once private freedoms were eliminated, public life became a farce, enacted by robots.

Once again, a popular American movie, although set in enemy territory, actually reflected the institutions and values people in the United States held most dear. The film's emphasis on women's spheres partly mirrored the female dominance in the audiences of 1943, but its acceptance as a film for export to troops and foreign allies suggested a general support for the message in *Hitler's Children*.[22]

In this film, the Nazi social order was threatening to men, forcing them to endure strict discipline—even torture at an early age—to mold them into acceptable citizens of the Third Reich. But there was glory attached to this role—uniforms, public displays, advancement through the ranks, power over others. For women, the fascist state offered a less enticing position. Females' choices were succinct and unbending: Either join the state as a supporter and eventual breeder of children or be sterilized and spend a brief life in a forced labor camp. Anna Muller, the rebel heroine in *Hitler's Children*, dramatized the warning issued by the Office of War Information: "If we lose the war, women will be driven back to their medieval status in society . . . Their lives, homes and families are endangered not only by the grim physical aspects of this total war, but also by the ideology of the enemy, which envisages a world wherein women will have few rights and fewer opportunities."[23]

A roaring bonfire—fueled by uniformed German boys' eager contributions of their country's literature—provides the first visual scene in *Hit-*

ler's Children. Blending with the crackling of the fire, patriotic music swells, sung by the same group of well-trained, rapt young men. As the camera pans a huge amphitheater of enchanted teenagers, the group rises to hail their fatherland, and at a Nazi officer's bidding, they willingly consecrate their lives to Hitler, "Our Savior, Our Führer."

As the camera lingers on the faces of these youthful, dedicated Nazis, a narrator's voice begins, immediately agreeing that the image before the audience (showing the total subjugation of the individual to the state) is difficult to believe. What makes it verifiable, the narrator entones, is a look at the past decade of German history, the era when "the indoctrination of the German young with Nazism" began.[24] Thus, as the film continues, viewers are taken back to 1933 when "Berlin was still a fairly pleasant place"; people could laugh and smile and the beer was wonderful.

Despite the scenes of gaiety and music, the narrator informs the audience, the influence of the Nazi educational machine was becoming apparent even in the first year of Adolph Hitler's chancellorship.[25] Although Berliners and foreigners continued their pleasures in biergartens, the children in the budding Third Reich were beginning their educations for death.

The effects of Nazi indoctrination are first visualized in a schoolyard, where an energetic fight is raging between students of the American Colony School and German boys of the Horst Wessel Academy. The struggle was begun by the aggressive Horst Wessel students, who are determined to show their superiority, but the adolescents of the American school show deftness and intelligence in their defense against the bullies. One of them, young Anna Muller (Bonita Granville), a pig-tailed blond, tries to repel tall, Aryan Karl Bruner's (Tim Holt) attack with a swing of her baseball bat. When he neatly sidesteps, grabbing the bat and preparing to tackle Anna, she yells, *"Heil, Hitler!"* Karl responds with a stiff Nazi salute, and Anna follows up her witty ploy by belting Karl in the stomach.[26]

The struggle between the youngsters is witnessed by Professor Nichols (Kent Smith), the film's narrator, who continues as movie-goers' guide throughout.[27] A gentle, scholarly figure, Professor Nichols is appalled by the violent fighting between the students of the two schools. He first tries to end the fisticuffs with reasonable pleas, but the belligerent Nazi boys will not listen and his students refuse to just take a beating. When he seeks the aid of the stern German officer in charge of the Horst Wessel Academy, the Nazi insists that they are witnessing a popular demonstration which must be allowed to run its course. Finally Professor Nichols ends the struggle by using the Nazis' tactics against them; when he barks military orders, the well-trained German boys immediately cease their fighting, and, swiftly forming ranks, they march with precision toward their school building.

Although the German students shown brawling in the movie's first scene are teenagers, the film suggests that they are still enormously vulnerable to the Nazis' indoctrination methods. The next sequence of the movie explores the reasons for these adolescents' ductility. While placing major responsibility for their malleability upon the planning and skill of the National Socialists' propaganda machine—one that "scientifically molded [children] into goose-stepping . . . freedom-hating Nazis"—the film also intimated that good Germans were available to Nazi doctrine because of the deep grudge they bore over the Treaty of Versailles.[28] Karl, Anna's youthful antagonist and the ambiguous hero in *Hitler's Children*, falls in this category.

As the camera follows the German boys into their classroom at the Horst Wessel Academy, Karl is shown sitting starkly upright at his desk, eyes glued to his uniformed teacher, a robot figure among identical others. Although his mind appears to wander as the sounds of laughter accompanying a baseball game at the American Colony School drift through the classroom windows, when he is called upon, Karl parrots his instructor's words perfectly, illustrating both his conditioning and his deep-felt convictions that Germans' birthrights include avenging the trickery of the Versailles Treaty and establishing a New Order in Europe.

In contrast to the regimented lectures of the Horst Wessel Academy, students in the American Colony School enjoy an informal, open style of learning, one punctuated by questions and discussions. At the same time Karl and his fellows are confined to desks and rote responses, students of the American School persuade Professor Nichols to teach their geography lesson out-of-doors, and the film's depiction of their heated debate over living space for Germany suggested that the American system of education allowed pupils to form their opinions autonomously, free from authoritarian pressures. Professor Nichols casually lounges among his circle of learners, listening instead of lecturing, and he carefully offers support to the youngsters who insist on an isolationist policy ("we could let everybody mind his own business"), as well as to Anna, who vigorously maintains that, "the whole world is everybody's business."

The attraction and strength of the flexible American system of education is underscored when Karl, intrigued by Anna's assertiveness, begins visiting her and finds Professor Nichols a receptive and benevolent mentor. Co-educational institutions are unheard of in Hitler's Germany, and Karl's attitudes reflect his sense of young women's inadequacies. "You play the piano very well for a girl," he remarks to Anna, and appears surprised when she reacts angrily to this attack on one of American women's traditional accomplishments. Anna softens, however, whenever she and Karl begin exchanging past histories. Discovering that Karl was born in the United States, Anna exclaims, "Why, you're hardly a German at all!" Karl refuses this description of himself, proclaiming affection and patriotism for Germany. Although Anna finds the Nazi influence over Karl repugnant, she accepts his feelings, for she was born in Germany of an American father, and her loyalties belong to America rather than the country of her birth.

For a brief interlude in the film, these teenagers of similar backgrounds form a strong bond under the tutelage of Professor Nichols. The three sing and frolic on picnics, the adolescents raptly listening as the professor reads Goethe on their excursions in the lovely hills south of Berlin. But the harsh disciplinary methods of the Third Reich intrude even into the beautiful countryside. One afternoon Anna's playful escape from Karl (whom she has just doused with water) is disturbed by her discovery of a young boy tied in spread-legged fashion on an anthill. After Anna removes the gag from his mouth, the 10-year-old explains that he is being punished for being caught as a spy in a war game. Anna is appalled and wishes to release the boy, but Karl insists that it is not their business to untie him, and the young patriot agrees. Begging to be left alone, the child (in obvious pain) contends that this is a test that he must pass in order to qualify for the Hitler Youth.[29] As Karl stoically salutes the boy, Anna runs away in tears, and the tenuous ties between her and Karl are severed.

As Anna and Karl go their separate ways, estranged by the Nazi influence over the young man, Professor Nichols explains the "storm that swept over Germany" during the late 1930s. Newsreel clips accompany Nichols' voice as he describes the aggressive actions of the Nazi state: the German withdrawal from the League of Nations, the remilitarization of the Rhineland, the annexation of Austria and a portion of Czechoslovakia, the alliance between Mussolini and Hitler. Lightning, thunder, and the rumble of tanks conclude the professor's narrative and as the camera returns to the American Colony School, which has "stood firm during the distressing time," viewers are treated to a patriotic scene of quiet simplicity, one that contrasts sharply with the documentary footage featuring Hitler's strident rhetoric and the marching German armies. A grown-up Anna, now a teacher, stands with her students, paying tribute to the flag of the United States. After her passionate recital of the Gettysburg Address, she leads the group in the singing of "America."

The freedom to conduct such foreign ceremonies has reached crisis proportions in the Third Reich, however. Gestapo officers intrude during the singing, bringing documents that certify their right to abduct all Jews, Poles, Lithuanians, and Germans from the American Colony School. Anna is included on the Nazis' list, despite her American citizenship, and neither her protest nor that of Professor Nichols has any impact on the stoney-eyed, cold Gestapo officer in charge—a thoroughly indoctrinated Karl Bruner. Anna is taken away with the other unfortunate victims of the Nazi dragnet to serve whatever purpose the Third Reich ordains, and a distraught Professor Nichols determines to rescue her.

Liberating Anna proves to be an impossible task, however, even for the resourceful scholar. The American Embassy has no influence in Nazi Germany; Anna's grandparents are too frightened to ask questions on her behalf; and even the brilliant, courageous journalist, Franz Erhardt (Lloyd Corrigan), is evasive and close-mouthed when Nichols visits him at home. Erhardt becomes more vocal during a later evening stroll, whispering not only Anna's whereabouts (a labor camp) but the reason for his silence in his home; Nazi educational methods now included children reporting their parents' conversations and those of visitors.

Newly cautious, Nichols continues his search for Anna surreptitiously, asking the minister of education for a tour of the labor camp in which she is interned so that he might study the new German methods. Dr. Graf (Hans Conried), a "gentleman whom it would be possible to greet as an equal," eagerly agrees to the professor's request, delighted with an opportunity to show off the scientific experiments of the New Order. The professor is referred to Colonel Henkel (Otto Kruger), a former Rhodes Scholar who fanatically supports the Nazi regime, and the colonel graciously offers his "perfect military aide," Karl Bruner, as Professor Nichols' guide.[30]

The American approaches the labor camp with trepidation, and nothing that he or the audience sees allays the collective fear of Nazi Germany. Every facet of living is regulated within the camp, not just during working hours, but through all hours of the day and night. No joking or friendly comments are permitted, and guards are ever-present to enforce the required robot behavior.

Such a constrained style of life can squelch the most vivacious person's spirit, as Anna's encounter with Professor Nichols soon illustrates. Because of Karl's influence (he is shown, at this point, to have retained a streak of sentimentality), Anna has been given an "easy" job in the labor camp; she is a public relations official, whose duty consists of explaining the virtues of the New Order to visitors. She performs her job admirably, showing no recognition when introduced to Professor Nichols and steelily insisting, when they have a private moment, that she has no desire to escape her present existence.

The influence of the labor camp appears to have changed Anna drastically. Severely dressed in a dark skirt, white blouse, and necktie, her hair pulled into a tight bun, she describes the work of the Third Reich in glowing terms. The professor responds in monosyllables, shocked at Anna's transformation and impatient with Karl's hovering presence. When the last stage of the tour is reached—a rest home for young, pregnant women—Professor Nichols can restrain himself no longer. When Karl remarks: "Despite foreign propaganda, you can see that these labor camps are not prisons," the professor retorts, "You mean that these girls are here voluntarily?" Karl insists: "They are drafted to serve just as men are in the Army, and they serve just as proudly." Anna breaks in, explaining the sexual customs in the New Order. Saturday night dances are regularly held, providing the opportunity for lovers to meet and "share the experience that makes them worthy of the Führer." When girls become pregnant and enter the rest home, Anna continues, "nothing is considered too good for them," for their children belong to the state. When the dismayed American points out that these young women's babies are illegitimate, his former star pupil calmly notes: "We have put aside these old superstitions."

The stunned professor cannot believe Anna's stoic acceptance of practices that abrogate her early upbringing and the standards of morality in the United States. Shaken, he presses the issue: "Does the state also offer these girls the alternative of a home and husband?" he asks. The German women are content with their choices, Anna counters, and she invites Nichols to talk with one of the camp's draftees to hear for himself. The young blond girl selected by the professor appears mystified by the American's queries about a home and husband. Sitting docilely in a lawn chair, savoring the sun, she tells the professor that the greatest possible honor for her is to bear a child for Hitler. Becoming animated as she thinks of her contribution to the Third Reich, the young woman expresses a desire for severe pain during her labor, so that she can feel "that I am going through a real ordeal for our Führer."

Nichols leaves the labor camp as rapidly as possible after this conversation, convinced that Nazi propaganda tactics have succeeded in poisoning the minds of all whom they have touched—including his precious Anna. But the young American citizen, whose birthright has been denied by the Germans, had reasons for her coldness to Professor Nichols. As he dejectedly leaves, she turns her fury on Karl, accusing him of trying to capture Nichols also and proclaiming her abiding hatred for the evil and rottenness inherent in Hitler's regime. Her vehement words shock and frighten Karl, who had believed her act more completely than had Professor Nichols. Karl swiftly insists that she must give the Nazi Party a fair chance, for he has recommended her for membership, and any rebellion on her part will be dangerous for both of them.

Anna, however, has nothing more to gain from playing a silent, obedient role. Convinced that the professor will now cease endangering himself by trying to rescue her, Anna begins her private revolt against the Nazis. Summoned to the minister of education's office to begin her studies for Party membership, Anna passionately declares to the high Nazi official, "I want no part of the diseased New World you're planning for mankind. And I'm ready to die to prove it."

The Nazi state does not offer a clean death to those who oppose it, however. As Karl's superior explains, "Dying is a luxury. In the New Order everyone must live and work." Thus Anna's punishment is a transfer from the staff of her camp to its labor corps, where she must become one of the regular Saturday night girls.

Convinced that death is a more attractive alternative than impregnation sanctioned by the state, Anna's rebellion assumes new forms. She refuses to salute the Führer and continually speaks out against the Nazis' political system. When Karl comes to the labor camp to check up on the recalcitrant woman whose conduct has placed his own career in jeopardy, he is told that Anna is "a dangerous agitator and no corrective measures seem effective."

Nonetheless, the Nazis are prepared to try one other experiment before forfeiting healthy Anna's possible contributions to the Third Reich. The audience discovers the nature of this treatment when Professor Nichols (whose determination to free "misguided" Anna has not abated) is invited on a further tour of the New Order's laboratories. Colonel Henkel serves as a guide on this occasion, for Karl's loyalties have been called into question, and the former Rhodes Scholar's words are directed to both men—testing their forbearance of Third Reich techniques in a most personal way.

The three men stroll into an observatory where windows look down into a huge operating room. As women are wheeled in and out beneath them, the colonel explains that they are watching a sterilization clinic in action. Here women who are unfit to have children by the state's decision are rendered incapable. Mostly this technique is used for weak or unstable girls, the colonel explains, but on occasion, the operation is performed on women whose political attitudes cause trouble. "It makes the women much quieter and more reasonable," Henkel observes. The American flinches, recognizing the thrust of the Nazi's message. Angered beyond control, he blurts, "You are barbarians, aren't you? Even the Rhodes scholars among you!" A silence falls as the professor stalks out, for Karl, who feels this experience as deeply as his former American friend, has learned to keep his own counsel in Nazi circles. Maintaining a poker face, he agrees with the criticisms Colonel Henkel levels against Nichols, but he privately determines to save Anna from the fate of the sterilization laboratories.

Karl's recognition of the tyranny of his government comes too late for either Anna's or his salvation. His attempts to help his childhood companion are circumscribed by his own limited imagination, and the power of the Nazi state. Seeking an outlet for Anna, he appears at the Saturday night dance at her labor camp, finding a sullen Anna bitterly repelling the overtures of eager young soldiers. Karl asserts his rank and claims Anna for his own pleasure, but he finds that Anna is as unreceptive to his offer of fatherhood as she was to other Nazi suitors, despite his confession of love. "Don't you see how wrong that is . . . how deceitful?" she cries, "It wouldn't be our child; it would be Hitler's!" Each generation must be responsible for future ones, the young woman insists, and she will die rather than produce more human fodder for the Nazi machine.

Leaving Karl in a bewildered, immobile state, Anna escapes into the forest, carrying the hopes of movie-goers with her. Up to this point in the film, the control of the Third Reich has been overwhelmingly impressive. The fanatic Nazis had indeed constructed a New Order—one that "suppress[ed] all individuality" and even placed "such private emotions as love and motherhood" under state supervision.[31] As Professor Nichols' and Anna's experiences showed, cooperation or negotiation with the arrogant tyrants of the Third Reich served no purpose. The only hope for people who resisted Nazi coercion was escape to a country outside Hitler's dominion.

The courageous rebel heroine in *Hitler's Children* attempts to reach such a sanctuary, but the oppressive noose of Nazi power is too strong and tight. The only haven Anna finds is a Catholic Church, where the sparse congregation tries to shield her when the Gestapo barges in. Their efforts are futile, however. Although the priest refuses to dismiss his parishioners, calmly stating, when the Secret Police point weapons at his head, "If to live what I think is to die, then let me die while I am still proud I am a German," Anna surrenders rather than see others killed. The Gestapo high command now decides that Anna will be used to discourage further resisters. Her punishment will be a public lashing, administered before the entire labor camp.

The ominous sound of drums is heard as a petrified Anna is dragged into the camp's courtyard and brutally handcuffed to a flagpole flying the Nazi swastika. As columns of women march in, assuming their places with rigid military precision, Anna's jailor roughly tears open the back of her blouse, shoving her into proper position for her whipping. As the roll of drums abruptly halts, a military car screeches into the courtyard, and Karl emerges, the order to proceed with Anna's punishment in his hand. He nods curtly to the Nazi executioner, who swiftly raises his whip, eyes glittering with pleasure. As the first crack of contact is heard, Anna grimaces in pain and sags to the ground.

The rebel heroine does not die in this scene, however. One strike of the lash on her bare flesh is all Karl can tolerate. His "better instincts assert themselves," and he attacks the flogger, wresting the whip from his hand and leaping to free Anna.[32] The couple has only a brief moment before the Gestapo moves in to arrest them, but it is sufficient time for them to exchange vows of love and undying fidelity.

As the movie rolls to its finish, the professor is shown waiting to board a plane at the Berlin airport, accomplishing the escape denied the unfortunate couple of mixed parentage. Nichols is avidly listening to a radio broadcast, for Karl and Anna have been granted a public trial. Colonel Henkel was persuaded to allow this open forum by Karl's assurance that he wished to confess and apologize, thus guaranteeing himself a soldier's funeral. As the professor boards the plane, Karl begins to speak, and suddenly Nichols recognizes familiar words. Karl is quoting Goethe, forbidden sentiments in the Third Reich. "Those who live for their faith shall behold it living," Karl recites. "If the whole world I once could see on free soil stand, with the people free, then to the moment might I say, linger awhile, so fair thou art. . . ." And, as Nichols stands frozen, realizing Karl's intent, the young man continues: "In Germany today . . . your education is an education for death. Long live the enemies of Nazi Germany!" As Karl finishes his rousing statement, gunshots reverberate through the radio's waves, and as the camera swiftly cuts to the Nazi courtroom, a fatally wounded Anna, her face glowing with pride, is shown crawling toward Karl, who has also been mortally injured. As the two dying persons clasp hands, the audience is reminded that there are "some things that outlast dictators."

Even as he weeps for the young persons he has known, Professor Nichols acknowledges their legacy. As he collapses in his seat on the plane that will lift him out of the heinous Nazi state, Nichols ponders the question: "Can we stop Hitler's children?" The movie suggests, in its final message, that Americans must "ask ourselves that question as we go home tonight."

By early 1943, government officials eager to recruit women for jobs in war plants and civilian businesses were concerned with the inadequacies of Hollywood features that presented limited images of women to the American public.[33] While federal spokespersons were urging females to take positions as bus drivers, grocery clerks, lumberjacks, waitresses, laundry workers, truck mechanics, and operatives in defense factories, *Meet the People*, an MGM movie of small appeal at the box-office, filmed a comedy sequence based on a working woman's incompetence in the kitchen. Distracted by other events, the heroine burns a pot roast. The scene earned the studio a rebuke from the Bureau of Motion Pictures. "The net of this routine," Bureau personnel remarked in a letter to MGM executives, is a reinforcement of "the Nazi propaganda line . . . that woman's place is really in the home."[34] Similarly, Columbia's *Blondie for Victory* was severely criticized for pursuing a comedy theme which suggested that "All of Blondie's voluntary activities are useless and detrimental to the smooth-running of the home, which in turn slows down the war work the men are doing."[35]

Movie producers could more directly aid the war effort, the OWI's Bureau of Motion Pictures advised in a manual offering guidelines to the industry, by showing women "driving taxis, serving as street car conductors, or filling-station operators," and adapting themselves "to living without husbands or sweethearts." Major studios were especially urged to not "cast Negroes always in menial or comic parts. . . . Like other minorities in America, [they] are doing their part toward winning the war."[36]

The image of competent, diverse women of all races and ethnic groups pushed by the BMP was not intended to denigrate the traditional spheres of women. On the contrary, homemakers were also vital persons according to the Bureau: "The housewife—individually—seldom thinks of herself as a very important element in the fibre of America," a publication of the Hollywood office of the Bureau maintained, "and yet, without the home life which she makes and preserves, we would have no strong, united nation." The crucial issue, according to these analysts of movie folklore, was that films distinguish between the freedoms that American women currently enjoyed and the position they would occupy in a fascist state. "A fascist world is a man's world," Fact Sheet No. 15 proclaimed. Women "would be denied higher education, the right to vote or hold office, the opportunity to find useful careers in business, science, or the arts. They would be chattels as they were in feudal times."[37]

By focusing on a young woman raised in an American environment but claimed by the Nazis because of her German ancestry, *Hitler's Children* dramatized what American females had to lose should the fascists be victorious in the "People's War." The gains that feminists had struggled for from the time of the Seneca Falls Convention of 1848 would be eliminated, of course, but even more devastating, according to the film, was women's potential loss of power within their traditional domains.[38] The policies of the Third Reich called for the destruction of the institutions and attitudes that both protected women and gave them status in society. Sexual liaisons—without the ties of love and marriage—were legitimized, and men were no longer expected to accept the responsibilities of fatherhood. Women bore their children for the state, which then denied them any rights to their offspring or any involvement in their upbringing. In the Third Reich, women no longer had the choice of a home and husband; they were drafted to breed and to work at menial tasks on command. Furthermore, the Nazis frowned upon religion and organized churches, refusing women access to a traditional area of solace and community influence.

Imbued with American ideals of freedom, Anna Muller found such a limited existence intolerable. In contrast to the German girls who had been indoctrinated to accept the Führer's wishes, the rebel heroine in *Hitler's Children* had been educated to think for herself and to demand recognition for her ideas. As a young student in the American Colony School, Anna was shown to be intelligent, witty, and argumentative. These qualities earned her a diploma and an advancement to the position of instructor. Furthermore, Anna was one of several girls in the American Colony School, while the movie showed only German boys in the classroom at Horst Wessel.

The right to an education was only one of the differences the film emphasized between the opportunities available to American girls and their German counterparts. Anna was shown to be competent in skills learned outside of the classroom; she was an energetic baseball player, a skilled pianist, and an aficionada of the arts, capable of appreciating Goethe in her adolescence. As a young woman, Anna was poised, secure, able in leadership positions, and independent enough to handle herself in crisis situations while still thinking of others, such as Professor Nichols, before herself. *Hitler's Children* intimated that Anna, one of the professor's special proteges, was a kind of home-grown American product, flowering under the influence of the American Colony School while the young females of the Third Reich were indoctrinated into a position of passive slavery.

These early years of education were vastly important, according to the movie. As a young adult, Anna was both politically aware of the heinous implications of Hitler's regime and sufficiently courageous to resist the solicitous or the coercive methods employed by Nazi henchmen. When she was taken to a labor camp, the rebel heroine carefully maintained her silence until she could be sure that her fellow Americans would not be involved on her behalf. Then Anna, acknowledging that "there is no way out for me," took an uncompromising stand. Refusing to countenance the evil and rottenness of Nazi Germany, she struck out against her captors, assured that her own morality and ideals were superior to those of the fascist New Order.

The course of Anna Muller's gallant rebellion illuminated the lengths to which the Nazis were willing to go in order to smash all individuality in the Third Reich's citizenry. When Anna expressed her political views, "I want no part of the diseased New World you're planning for mankind," she was not granted her wish for a swift and dignified death. Instead the Nazis determined to break this recalcitrant woman, forcing her to accept a role in their fascist state.

The tactics the fascists used to coerce Anna struck at the very core of the freedoms that American women were seen to possess in 1943, raising a furor among film critics and theater patrons alike. *Hitler's Children* "is a vital and angry document, dedicated to the purpose of making American audiences angry, too," *The Hollywood Reporter* noted.[39]

No more vulnerable spot existed in the American psyche than an attack on motherhood and women's rights in general, according to the movie. Americans flocked to see Anna's journey through oppression, and they watched in horror as Anna was denied the opportunity to pursue her career, and later was sent to a labor camp for articulating her political beliefs. Most gruesome, however, was the fascists' insistence that Anna join the pool of Saturday night girls and bear a child for the Führer and, when faced with Anna's stern resistance, the Nazi's threat to sterilize the young woman.

Americans could also find other ways in which Anna's freedoms were abridged. She was, for example, denied the protection of the man who loved her. The hostile regime of Nazi Germany had created an environment in which "even such private emotions as love and motherhood are supervised so that the state is served."[40] In the Third Reich, Anna and Karl could maintain the traditional ties of romantic love only by forfeiting their lives.

The list of horrors to which Anna Muller was subjected in *Hitler's Children* revealed the American folklore about the worst things that could happen to women. A public whipping was very high on the list, but forced breeding and sterilization were without doubt the most ghastly. According to the film, American females' most basic liberties included the right to a husband and home of one's choice, and the opportunity to have children free of state interference.[41]

Anna died rather than accept a lifestyle that precluded such choices. In *Hitler's Children* a young woman shouldered the burden of guarding society's ethics, and she willingly gave her life in the cause. In the folklore of the country, Anna behaved in proper fashion. Her tragic end spoke to the wickedness of the Nazis, of course, a popular theme in war movies produced at this time. Anna's and Karl's deaths, however, also gave reinforcement to the value of romantic love, marriage, and the family. A society which outlawed these institutions, the film suggested, was not one worth inhabiting.

The rebel heroine in *Hitler's Children* fought and died for the ideals of a country she had seen only briefly. In *Behind the Rising Sun*, a movie set in totalitarian Japan, an Oriental heroine watches her American-educated sweetheart metamorphose into a cruel, fanatic soldier of the Imperial Forces. Although Tama was a Japanese citizen who had never visited the United States, she realized the ethics worthy of defense more accurately than her misguided fiance, Taro Seki.

Behind the Rising Sun (RKO, 1943)

RKO's *Behind the Rising Sun* was the only best-selling feature movie of the war years to offer Americans a vision of ordinary people's lives in Imperial Japan. Based on a book of the same title by correspondent James R. Young, the film purported to tell "a true-to-life story of Japan . . . based on actual facts, verified and authenticated." Although reviewers challenged the credibility of the movie—one suggesting that it was "an 88-minute jag of ferocious anti-Japanese propaganda"—Nelson Poynter of the OWI's Bureau of Motion Pictures listed the film among eight 1943 productions that "tend[ed] to give a serious interpretation of the enemy."[42]

Director Edward Dmytryk's and adaptor Emmet Lavery's second box-office success for RKO (the first was *Hitler's Children*) sought to explain the Japanese enthusiasm for fascism and a war of conquest. Totalitarian-minded officials are shown at work during the 1930s, assassinating peace-oriented government figures and creating an army of ruthless, dedicated soldiers. The film earned praise from the Bureau of Motion Pictures mainly because it eschewed stereotypical "Jap-hating" and attempted a depiction of the enemy based on the BMP's "Yardstick for War Pictures." This bulletin urged movie producers to "try to make the people understand that their enemy is neither a handful of Axis leaders around Hitler, Mussolini and Tojo . . . nor all the German, Italian and Japanese people. The enemy is many people infected with a poisonous doctrine of hate, of might making right."[43]

Although *Behind the Rising Sun* met the BMP's standards more fully than other low-budget movies, the film also suggested that good Japanese could cure themselves of the poisonous infection endemic in their country. As one scene moves to another in this "grueling patchwork of cinematrocities," all the noble Japanese characters renounce their Emperor as well as the fascist government, choosing either an honorable death or work in the underground rather than die-hard allegiance to their nation. While soldiers of the Imperial Forces might be immoral and barbaric and beyond the reach of ethics, the movie implied that by 1943, statesmen and ordinary Japanese citizens were realizing the extent to which they had been manipulated by an evil government. "Destroy us as we have destroyed others," pleads a major character at the film's end. "Destroy us before it's too late." *Newsweek*'s reviewer called this "a sound sentiment . . . devoutly to be wished," but he also noted, rather sarcastically, that its occurrence was "hardly likely to be aided from within the land of the Rising Sun."[44]

The popularity of *Behind the Rising Sun* suggests that war-conscious Americans were quite willing to spend some of their rare leisure time trying to figure out, in *The New Yorker*'s critic's words, "what makes the Japanese people the strange lot they are today." RKO's "B" grade film certainly offered a palatable answer to wartime movie-goers. No Oriental persons appeared in the film and the "unconvincing makeups and spurious accents" of American actors encouraged any extant stereotyping in viewers' minds. Furthermore, Japanese patterns of living, whether the traditions attached to family or the ceremonies associated with groups such as the Samurai, were consistently denigrated in the box-office hit. Although the film was advertised as a study of Japanese homelife, what emerged on the screen was a paean to the superiority of American ways.[45]

At the movie's beginning the young hero, Taro Seki, was a totally Americanized Cornell graduate. He had returned to his father's house, but he had imported American ways, preferring handshakes to formal bows and insisting on bathing alone, loudly singing "Hail to Cornell" while splashing in the tub. As Seki was transformed into a "child-bayonetting" soldier of the Imperial Forces, he lost his Western mannerisms, adopting the corrupt customs of his homeland. Seki's eventual death was portrayed as a cleansing action more than a tragedy. Even as Taro's father mourned his son, he expressed the hope that "the people of Japan might redeem themselves before . . . a civilized world."

In contrast to Taro Seki, the Japanese heroine of the movie, Tama, remained enchanted with American values throughout the feature. A person of Japan's lower class, she found a chance for upward mobility as a secretary in an American engineering firm. Her day-by-day contacts with Clancy O'Hara, a United States citizen, convinced her of the backwardness of Japanese customs as well as the malevolence of the fascists who controlled the country. For Tama, neither the old empire nor the Japanese New Order offered reasonable alternatives. As a woman, she had to wait and work for the "Japan that is yet to be born"—a nation, according to the film, that replicated the United States in significant ways.

By the summer of 1943, when *Behind the Rising Sun* was released in American theaters, Allied military forces were clearly on the offensive in the Pacific. The famous Battle of Midway, which historians have seen as the turning point in the Asian theater of war, was more than a year in the past and marine and naval campaigns were underway "to tighten the noose around Japan." The Japanese islands had also been penetrated in April of 1942 when Lieutenant Colonel James H. Doolittle had led an audacious raid of 16 B-25 Bombers over Tokyo. Although the Japanese were proving themselves tenacious and clever enemies, by 1943 Americans had reason for optimism regarding the eventual outcome of the war.[46]

The beginning scenes of the RKO best-seller reinforced viewers' feelings of confidence in American prowess. As the tinny sounds of Oriental music are heard, the camera focuses on the ruins of a bombed home in Tokyo, a reminder of the Doolittle Raid. The figure moving within is shown, in close-up, to be an old woman, alone and bereft of any comfort other than her shrine to the Emperor. As she kneels in worship, softly muttering wishes for the days before Pearl Harbor, the audience receives the impression of a defeated people, shoring themselves for an ultimate disaster.

The mood is accentuated as the camera shifts to pan the faces of a long column of obedient, stoic Japanese men. These persons are identified quickly as the sons, fathers, or male relatives of Japanese soldiers killed in combat. They have come to claim, ceremoniously, the ashes of their war dead, and their numbers alone speak to the effectiveness of American military maneuvers.

The line of impassive men becomes more personal as one figure is highlighted. Ryo Seki (J. Carrol Naish), immaculate in dress and manners, steps forward to receive the urn containing his son's remains. Seki, observing protocol, shows no emotion, but the camera follows him back to his affluent home, where in his quiet study, he sits in traditional Japanese posture and dress, and begins a letter to his dead son, Taro, seeking to explain "the manner of his son's living and dying."

Ryo Seki's recollections provide the framework for *Behind the Rising Sun*'s history of the fascist takeover in Japan and the subsequent effects of the Japanese war of conquest. In the 1930s, the Seki family was upper class, comfortably wealthy and prestigious because of ancestry and Ryo's position as a newspaper owner and publisher. As the patriarch of the Seki family thinks back, he recalls the violent scenes of the early 1930s, when fascist soldiers began their intimidation of street crowds and the assassination of liberals. The audience sees pandemonium ruling the cities and statesmen attacked and murdered in their beds, one gasping in a dying moan, "If to want peace in Asia is to be a foreigner, then I must die a foreigner."

At the time of the fascist ascendancy, Seki recalls, Taro was just returning from the United States, a successful and ambitious graduate of Cornell University. "It might have been a day out of yesterday that was overtaking me," Seki reminisces, for he too had been educated in America. And as Seki purges himself of grief, writing his memoirs to his dead son in preparation for his own death by suicide, the scene dissolves to picture Taro's homecoming—a buoyant, happy occasion.

A chauffeured limousine crawls slowly through the masses of people thronging the wharves of Tokyo's harbor, stopping finally before a huge passenger liner that has just docked. As a formally attired Ryo Seki emerges from the car (looking suspiciously like the Japanese ambassadors Americans saw in newsreels at the time of Pearl Harbor), his son, Taro (Tom Neal) leaps down the gangplank, shouting, "Gee, Pop, it's good to see you!" Mr. Seki responds to his son's boisterous greeting with a quiet, traditional bow, and Taro halts apologetically, confessing "Sorry, Dad, I forgot how they do things in Japan." Ryo smiles indulgently, accepting the "Americanisms" adopted by his son. Later at home, Taro's family shows the same tolerance, praising the young graduate's moustache and Western haircut and only showing alarm with Taro's ideas and manners when he speaks of "striking out on his own." Taro's grandmother is especially mystified and aggravated by Taro's American-inspired goal. "In Japan the family is everything," she chides. Taro's duty is now to enter the family newspaper business, training himself diligently to be his father's successor.

Taro's years at Cornell have seemingly been more influential than the preceding ones in his Japanese home. As the story progresses, Taro, determined to use his knowledge of American technology, seeks a job in a Tokyo-based United States firm, the O'Hara Engineering Company. Clancy O'Hara (Don Douglas), a muscular Irishman, is impressed with the ambitious Japanese youth who speaks eloquently of his desire "to build the things that Japan needs to end the human destruction" caused by earthquakes, fires, and floods. But O'Hara also confesses to Taro his fears about the political situation in Japan, especially since the Seki newspaper has recently endorsed anti-foreigner policies. Taro blithely assures O'Hara that the fascist influence in Japan is only a phase, one that will rapidly pass when his people learn more about American ways. O'Hara's secretary, Tama (Margo), a tall, attractive brunette, substantiates Taro's claim. Her cool, efficient demeanor slips quickly when she hears that Taro has attended college in the United States, and she plies him with child-like questions: "Are the girls in offices all as pretty as Ginger Rogers? Can you do just what you want to do . . . whether born in a log cabin or not?" Taro is delighted with Tama's naiveté and interest and the sparks between the two indicate that a romantic involvement has begun.

The optimism in O'Hara's office is swiftly undercut as *Behind the Rising Sun* moves viewers to Ryo Seki's imposing, plush newspaper building. Seki is shown in conference with his friend, Boris, a Russian secret agent. The publisher is trying to convince his Soviet acquaintance that the Emperor can hold firm against the fascists, but Boris remains skeptical. "Remember," he advises Seki, "the Chinese saying: 'Man who chooses to ride tiger must ride where tiger is going.' " Seki counters the Russian's words with skillful courtesy, pointing out that the fascists in Japan are not entirely wrong. "Who holds the heartland of Asia holds the world," he asserts. "And Japan is best suited to that role." Ushering Boris from his luxurious suite, Seki appears to discover a moment of truth within himself. And in a later conversation with his son, he admits the substance of his revelation, completely dropping his mask of suavity. The fascists' emphasis on national pride and racial superiority is *beneficial* to the Emperor's goals, Seki proclaims. Japan must be allowed to assume its rightful, dominant place in the community of nations, and the white man must grasp the fact that he is a minority throughout the world. Rage appears to consume Seki as he speaks of racial slights against his people, and the calm businessman is replaced by a fanatic believer. "The time shall come," Seki snarls, "when we shall see who is the master and who is the slave."

Ryo Seki's discourse was the most sympathetic account of Japanese aims that *Behind the Rising Sun* offered. Well-meaning, American-educated Japanese were shown to be impatient and dissatisfied with their nation's secondary position. These feelings were exploited easily by right-wing elements in the nation, the film implied, as were resentments harbored by the Japanese on the racial issue.[47]

Evoking a thoughtful consideration of "the Japs'" goals in Asia before Pearl Harbor was not a strong priority in this wartime film, however. The fanaticism that consumed Seki as he symbolically crushed a white chess piece in his fist while speaking of "masters" and "slaves" seems calculated to move viewers' attention from interest in Japanese ambitions to fear of an "unreasonable yellow horde." The film intimated that a "white-hating" extremist dwelt within every citizen of the Japanese Empire, emphasizing the inevitability of racial conflict and reinforcing American movie-goers' apprehensions about "the yellow peril."

In contrast to blanket Japanese white-hating, Americans living in Japan in the 1930s are shown as tolerant and accepting where race is concerned, much more involved in assessing individuals' abilities than making group racial judgments. O'Hara employs Taro in his business, despite Ryo's objections, because the young man is a talented, well-prepared engineer. And O'Hara teases Tama about her interest in Taro in the classic style of American bosses who protect their secretaries until they are sure that the right man has come along. Although the Americans featured in the movie express concern about the political situation in Japan, they are shown to have close friendships with Japanese families and to be outgoing and approachable to everyone they meet.[48]

The Americans' acceptance of the Japanese on individual rather than racial terms seemed to encourage criticism of the strange institutions in Japanese society. O'Hara and some of his cronies from the United States, accompanied by the faithful Taro, provided the American audience with an insider's view of the institution apparently most foreign to movie-goers—the geisha house—in the film's next scenes.

As the sequence begins, the camera finds O'Hara in a bar in Tokyo, drinking and gambling with Caucasian and Japanese friends. His off-work fun is interrupted when Sarah Brayton (Gloria Holden), an attractive, ebullient, brunette correspondent, spies him. The American newspaper-woman and O'Hara are old friends and, at this stage of political unrest, Sarah would like the relationship to be something more. She has been called to cover Japan's beginning military action in China, and afraid of the approaching holocaust, she pleads with O'Hara to marry her. "I know it isn't womanly and all that," Sarah says frankly, "but we've known each other for a long time now and I'm going away for a long time too. . . . Well, there's no harm in a girl trying, is there?"

There appears to be no harm in Sarah's proposal (except to her ego) but there is no success either. O'Hara nervously bolts with his male companions, entering the sanctuary of a geisha house, an institution, he has informed Sarah, that is "no place for ladies—not nice ladies anyway." Paradoxically, as the American men and Taro play poker in the tiny room that furnishes O'Hara refuge from an "aggressive American woman," they comment in maudlin fashion about the plight of women in Japan. First, they pride themselves on their conduct—a baseball coach, Lefty (Robert Ryan) remarking with a leer, "You don't usually come to a geisha house to play cards." And they label the geisha girls who ask about their comfort "little children . . . to whom life is very simple." Yet women in geisha houses are very fortunate in these men's opinion. They are favored prostitutes, the Americans explain, while thousands of Japanese girls are sold into slavery of a more brutal sort. "And don't forget," one card-player drunkenly insists, "the forgotten women of Japan, the wives and mothers who are the real drudges in this slave society."

Taro is deeply impressed by his party-companions' comments on the treatment of women in Japan. Accepting their judgment, he determines to breach convention and marry Tama, elevating her to upper-class status despite her peasant background. When Taro proposes to Tama (on a softly lighted dance floor—a favorite setting in films of the early forties), she is willing but troubled. It is not the "Japanese way," she frets, and Taro's family will be displeased. Her confident fiance insists that he can arrange everything. Tama is not to worry her pretty head. She must concentrate instead on becoming "housebroken," which Taro defines in behavioral terms as "never yelling at baseball games" and "never correcting him." Tama demurely agrees to these conditions, and the couple embraces.

Violence intrudes on this mellow scene, however, as radio news of Japanese successes in China evokes excited responses among restaurant patrons, especially one soldier who leaps into battle stance, his sword cutting the air in a "Samurai Dance of Victory." Both Tama's and Taro's faces register horror as the soldier cavorts, but a swift glance at the dancer's audience convinces them of their own impotence. Their fellow citizens are enjoying their nation's successes in military action, and any dissenter would be dealt with harshly.

As the war effort in China forces more discipline on Japanese society, Taro and Tama find their opportunity for a private existence curtailed. Taro gamely confronts his father with his marriage plans and encounters a flat refusal. The social structure of Japan is the basis of its strength, Ryo explains to his rebellious son. While Japan must use the technological and military tools of the twentieth century, the social arrangements from the past must also be preserved. "On the bottom of the heap are the people—the patient millions who toil in the fields and the factories and who are content to live on nothing," Ryo muses. "On the top of the heap are the great families who own the fields and the factories, the Army and the Navy—even the Emperor himself. In between there is practically nothing." Ryo urges Taro to accept his ordained position in society and to forget his democratic ideals of marriage. His son is not convinced, however, and he angrily leaves his father's home, ready to sever his relationship with his family and go it alone.

As Taro closes the door on his ancestral home, he finds an emissary from his government awaiting him with draft papers in hand. Cutting the ties of homeland as well as family proves too formidable a task even for

Americanized Taro. He joins the Imperial Forces, leaving Tama and the confusion at home for a clearly-defined military career in China.

The next scenes in *Behind the Rising Sun* show Taro Seki's departure for China to have been a crucial decision. Pride keeps him from communicating with his father, and pride keeps Ryo from accepting word of his son through Tama. Without guidance and constant support, Taro becomes just another officer in the Japanese military. Taro's degeneration is depicted through correspondent Sarah Brayton's eyes.

Sarah is covering the story of the Japanese takeover of yet another Chinese city. As she wanders through the crowded streets, she observes the panic of the defeated Chinese, and her face reflects both sympathy and fear. Suddenly Japanese soldiers appear and roughly thrust her off the sidewalk, slapping her when she protests their conduct. Reacting to violent treatment, Sarah cowers in her hotel room, watching the street activities through a small window. Disgust swamps her features when she sees the Japanese conquerors giving opium to Chinese children as well as adults. Then her face brightens. She has seen a familiar figure. Taro is among the Japanese officers in the occupation force. Sarah casts aside her apprehension and runs into the street, just in time to see Japanese soldiers under Taro's command snatching babies from their mothers' arms and disposing of them with bayonets before gang raping their mothers. When Sarah approaches Taro, she encounters a stick figure, a remote commander who recognizes her only vaguely and insists that she return to her hotel room. Sarah does—chagrined that she had trusted Seki to do something.

The camera leaves an embittered Sarah at this point, following Taro back to his quarters, where the audience is given access to the young officer's real feelings. Taro's experiences in China have convinced him that his nation's military is out of control and his own participation in Japanese atrocities has left him with deep feelings of self-hatred. He clings to his memories of Tama and his hopes for their marriage: "The world may change," he writes, "but you and I will never change." Even as Taro writes, the screams of Chinese women are heard outside his quarters. As he jumps up, automatically responding to the cries for help, he is suddenly struck with a terrible awareness of his own powerlessness. He can do nothing to halt the Japanese war machine; he is, in fact, a part of it and dreaming of a future with Tama is nothing more than a convenient escape. Thus, under duress, Taro Seki sheds his old values, repressing the American influence in his life and the honorable ways of traditional Japanese culture. For better or worse, Taro pledges himself to the goals of fascist Japan.

In Tokyo, the Seki family has also undergone a transformation. Determined to end the estrangement between Taro and her son, Ryo's mother suggests a way to reconcile honor and tradition with Taro's love for his fiancee. A friend of Ryo's, a member of their same class, will adopt Tama, making her "as good as we are." A reluctant Ryo finally accepts his mother's plan, particularly when the tiny woman endorses the marriage herself, pointing out that "Tama will make him a very good wife and that is all that matters."

When Taro returns to Tokyo on leave, O'Hara, who is still convinced that his nation and the Japanese will work out their differences, insists on hosting a celebration for the Seki family. Champagne toasts to Ryo, the new minister of propaganda in the recently formed Cabinet of Prime Minister Hideki Tojo, and to Taro, have just begun when a haggard Sarah Brayton drops in on the O'Hara party. Although she is smartly dressed in a fashionable suit, Sarah is exhausted emotionally and very angry with Taro and all Japanese soldiers. "Very pretty," she shrills to the guests who stand with upraised glasses, "but you're forgetting something, aren't you? Why don't you drink to the memory of the children Taro Seki murdered in China?" The distinguished group offers a collective gasp at Sarah's words while Taro's face convulses in rage. O'Hara attempts to placate Sarah, but she will accept no comfort from a man who consorts with the enemy. As she stalks out proudly, Taro starts after her, his desire for retribution clear. O'Hara intervenes, cajoling Taro with soft words, "After all, she's a woman. Sometimes women make mistakes." Taro furiously rejects O'Hara's overture, slapping his face when the American continues to block his exit. O'Hara is stunned by Taro's action, but his expression swiftly reveals an awakening sense of the changes in his former employee. The buoyant, idealistic college graduate he hired four years ago has become a sadistic officer of Imperial Japan. When Taro demands satisfaction for Sarah's insult, O'Hara readily agrees.

The two principals in conflict, Taro and O'Hara, are not allowed to fight directly because of Ryo's position in the government. Instead they choose deputies, and American boxing skills—in the person of Lefty— are pitted against jujitsu expertise. The fight is "a gaudy bit of sensationalism," in the movie, "as savage as anything in the history of screen roughhouse." Yet, for audiences in 1943, the "boxer-wrestler battle symbolized the U.S.-Jap war." Significantly, when the camera dwells on the face of the jujitsu master (Mike Mazurki) in his moments of triumph in the long, brutal fight, his expressions convey an orgiastic pleasure, seemingly derived from inflicting pain as well as winning. Lefty and spectator, O'Hara, on the other hand, show no enthusiasm—even in their final victory. Their manner suggests victimized people who find no joy in battle, but recognize the need to win and therefore furnish the required skills and endurance.[49]

The fight between Lefty and Taro's deputy forces O'Hara to reconsider his position in the country he has adopted for 20 years. Although he has sustained his (and America's) honor, he has also created a lasting enmity with Taro and the military power he represents. O'Hara's conclusions are verified by a visit from Ryo Seki, who now recants his allegiance to the fascists. "I have made a mistake," he admits. "We are not fit to rule the world." Seki predicts that Japan will be at war with the United States soon—"a war," he sorrowfully projects, "that Japan will win." O'Hara must leave the islands quickly, Seki advises, for he has seen the future in his son, a person "who wants to kill for the sheer joy of killing."

Tama has not arrived at this conclusion about Taro. Her affection for him and her desire for an idyllic future persuade her that a few days in the country will return her fiance to his old self. The two set out by car to visit Tama's parents at her family's farm, and Taro's actions do mirror the optimistic youth who teased Tama years ago in O'Hara's office. When the couple arrive at their destination (the farm looking very much like one in Iowa), Tama is happy and serene, unaware of her parents' worried glances until their dinner conversation becomes evasive. When pressed, Tama's parents admit that their youngest daughter, her favorite sister, has been sold into prostitution. Tama sadly accepts her parents' rationale. War taxes had forced them to this measure; it was their daughter or the farm, but she becomes incensed when Seki remarks, "Your sacrifice makes you worthy of the Emperor." As Tama's face clouds with rebellion, news of Pearl Harbor interrupts the family meal. Shock and fear dart across the peasants' faces, but Taro Seki is delighted. "This is it! The White War!" he exults. And commanding a stunned Tama to hurry, Taro chides, "This is no time for personal considerations. When the Emperor calls the individual counts for nothing."

The war that good-hearted but misguided Ryo Seki had predicted had come, and the lives of all the characters in *Behind the Rising Sun* finally reach a denouement. The Americans, Clancy O'Hara, Sarah, and Lefty, are consigned to jail while Tama is urged to implicate them in espionage activities. She refuses, but her resistance and theirs, even under painful torture, prove nothing to the distrustful Japanese (O'Hara is shown being burned by a cigarette, Lefty is pictured dangling from ropes binding his wrists, and the camera focuses on Sarah's quaking hands as a knife is thrust toward her fingernails). When Colonel Taro Seki arrives to denounce the lot—Tama included—their deaths at the hands of the enemy appear certain, a situation affirmed by O'Hara when he finally concedes his bachelorhood and proposes to Sarah.

The Americans and their dedicated friends do not die, however. The Doolittle Raid evokes enough panic and confusion for Ryo's surreptitious release of the prisoners whom he then offers safe conduct out of Japan. Only Tama refuses, insisting that she must stay to help create the "Japan that is yet to be born."

Taro is killed defending his homeland in the same daring raid that saved the Americans whom he had condemned to death. After his plane is shown flaming to earth, the film returns viewers to Ryo's quiet study, where he gazes with sorrow at the urn containing his son's ashes. The former minister of propaganda has completed his letter to his son and satisfied with his probe of Taro's living and dying, he now explains his own decision for suicide. "I do not die for the Emperor, a near-sighted, little man on a white horse," Seki emotes. "I die for the repudiation of the Emperor and everything he has stood for. I die for the hope . . . that the people of Japan may . . . redeem themselves before . . . a civilized world." And as Ryo poises his sword for its fatal plunge into his heart, he prays: "To whatever Gods there are left in the world—Destroy us as we have destroyed others. Destroy us before it's too late."

"The American war movie was probably more important as an historical phenomenon than as an artistic achievement," Ken D. Jones and Arthur McClure wrote in 1973. Their evaluation certainly fits RKO's best-selling *Behind the Rising Sun*. The film has no aesthetic appeal—its convoluted plot leaves the viewer mystified while the characters are drawn in flat dimensions, evoking little negative or affectionate feeling.[50]

Behind the Rising Sun is significant as a piece of historical evidence. Box office receipts placed this badly-made film among the most popular of 1943, suggesting that wartime Americans were very curious about their "mysterious, yellow enemy" and that they were pleased enough by the movie's portrayal of Japanese society to pass the word on to neighbors and friends.[51]

The reasons for American viewers' enthusiasm for *Behind the Rising Sun* are not hard to decipher. Through the characters of Ryo Seki and his son, Taro, the audience experienced the fascists' rise to power in Japan. They saw how good people (that is, American-influenced Japanese) were infected by a doctrine of hate, and they witnessed the destruction of these same characters—the younger in air battle with Americans, the older in remorse for his country's evil stance against the United States. The message conveyed by these portraits was reassuring. Both the Allied armed forces and American ideals were powerful enough to conquer the enemy.

Behind the Rising Sun also offered soothing comments on the issue of race. Americans such as O'Hara and Sarah Brayton were shown to be fair-minded and unprejudiced, eager to help the people of a "backward" culture enter a technological age. Their switch to an anti-Japanese position came slowly and reluctantly, forced by the extreme actions of the military or political rulers in Japan. Moreover, the remarks of the Sekis, both eager at different points in the film to engage in a white war, exonerated Americans from racism. In RKO's film, it was the Japanese who thought in racial terms.

The scriptwriters of *Behind the Rising Sun* (who were quite attuned to popular attitudes if movie profits can be believed) created a movie which thoroughly reinforced extant American opinions. The responsibility for the war in the Pacific was placed entirely on the Japanese, and the anti-yellow feelings shared by most Americans of the time were shown to be proper, defensive ones—natural reactions to a race with aggressive designs to crush the white man.

It is not surprising to find a well-liked movie of the war years encouraging and rationalizing the hostility that Americans felt toward "the yellow peril." It is revealing, however, that officials in the Bureau of Motion Pictures, who rather evenly championed the cause of black people during the BMP's brief existence, raised no objections to the racial content of *Behind the Rising Sun*. Evidently these liberal government spokesmen were content to allow the notion to linger that all Japanese—whether enemies of another nation or citizens of the United States—had "brought their condition upon themselves." Americans of Japanese descent (who by 1943 were almost entirely incarcerated in detainment camps in the United States) received no mention in *Behind the Rising Sun*.[52]

The movie did convey the impression that some "good Japs" existed, however. The heroine of RKO's feature, Tama, was a progressive-minded new woman, who rebelled against Japanese tradition while also consistently opposing the New Order in Imperial Japan. Significantly, she was the only Japanese character in *Behind the Rising Sun* who emerged as noble, virtuous, and *alive* in the end. Both male Sekis, whether committed to fascism or tainted by its pull, were scheduled to die in this bestseller. Tama, on the other hand, seemed gifted with an uncanny ability to distinguish between right and wrong.

The film suggested that the kernel of Tama's wisdom lay in her early upbringing among Americans. Her family was helped by the Red Cross during a natural disaster, and she later attended a missionary school. As she grew to maturity, other Americans influenced Tama—her boss, O'Hara, and correspondent Sarah Brayton, who courageously denounced the Japanese at a public gathering.

Yet the movie intimated, by Tama's intelligence and survival, that the issue was deeper than a Japanese woman's grasp of American principles. *Behind the Rising Sun* suggested that women's intuition inevitably led females to a universal understanding, the kind of union expressed by a fictitious American housewife in a script entitled, "Main Street Calling":[53]

> Women know about things like . . .
> Blood and sweat and tears.
> There's a lot we don't say . . .
>
> But I could try to say one thing:
>
> Maybe, when this part is over,
> The dreadful, killing part,
> If the men would let us try
> Along with them,
> When the fixing-up begins,
> The mending, the healing, the new way, the setting-in-order,
> The building, the teaching, the comforting . . .
> We know about those things.
>
> Maybe then the children can enjoy the world . . .
> It's a beautiful place, in itself . . .
> And they won't have to choose
> Between slavery and slaughter
> Again, ever again.
>
> Anyway, we could try, because
> There are no boundary lines
> Among women.

The sentiment expressed by the housewife-heroine in "Main Street Calling" was not a new idea that emerged suddenly during the World War II years. The perception that women of all nations and races were by nature more peaceful than men had been introduced for public debate in the early twentieth century. Some feminists of that era used the argument to promote women's inclusion in public life, claiming that females' "moral superiority" would lead them to exercise power more compassionately than bellicose men. And pacifism replaced the suffrage cause in many women's lives after 1920, creating substantial membership lists for organizations such as the National Conference on the Cause and Cure of War and The Women's International League for Peace and Freedom.[54]

Although the efforts of these peace advocates of the inter-war years did not prevent another world conflict, *Behind the Rising Sun* suggested that women and peace were linked together in the public mind. Both Tama and Sarah, women of different nationalities, were horrified by war; each lamented its coming and each took an open stand against its atrocities. The fact that neither was a mother or domestic female (although both wished these roles in their futures) accentuated the universalism of women's inherent pacifism and moral superiority as well as the ethnocentrism of this type of film. Nevertheless, the popularity of *Behind the Rising Sun* leaves a record of the perceptions dominant in the public consciousness of the mid-war years. According to the film, even American-influenced Japanese men were susceptible to fascist propaganda. Under these circumstances, Americans had no choice but to destroy them. Japanese women, on the other hand, were eager to end their oppression, and towards this end they recognized and appreciated the values of the United States.

Mirroring popular American attitudes, *Behind the Rising Sun* subscribed to the idea of women's intuitive virtue. Since "no boundary line among women existed," through the aegis of women like Tama, a new—safe—Japan "could be born."

Plate 1.   Joan Leslie in *Sergeant York*.

Plate 2.   Barbara Stanwyck and Gary Cooper in *Meet John Doe*.
(Courtesy of Columbia Pictures Television.)

Plate 3.   Greer Garson and Teresa Wright in *Mrs. Miniver*.
(Courtesy of MGM, Loew's. Copyright © 1942 Loew's Inc.
Copyright renewed 1969 by Metro-Goldwyn-Mayer Inc.)

Plate 4.   Paul Henreid, Ingrid Bergman, and Humphrey Bogart in *Casablanca*.
(Copyright © 1943. Warner Bros. Pictures, Inc. Renewed 1970 United Artists Television. All Rights Reserved.)

Plate 6.   Margo, Don Douglas, and Gloria Holden in *Behind the Rising Sun*.
(Courtesy of RKO General Pictures.)

Plate 8. Hattie McDaniel, Shirley Temple, Joseph Cotten, and
Claudette Colbert in *Since You Went Away*.
(Courtesy of Vanguard Films. Copyright © 1948 Vanguard Films,
Inc.)

Plate 9.   Women in combat, as portrayed in *So Proudly We Hail*.
(Courtesy of Paramount Pictures. Copyright © 1943 Paramount
Pictures, Inc.)

Plate 10.   Claudette Colbert in *So Proudly We Hail*.
(Courtesy of Paramount Pictures. Copyright © 1943 Paramount
Pictures Inc.)

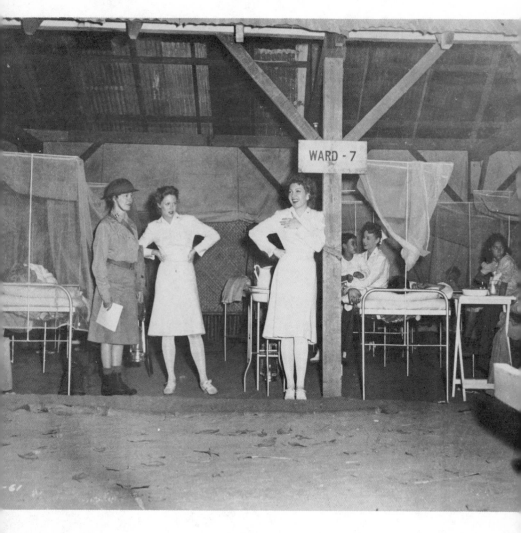

Plate 11.   Dying marine in *Guadalcanal Diary* illustrates the importance of family to soldiers in combat. (Courtesy of 20th Century-Fox.)

4

Heroines on the Home Front

Few war movies produced during World War II gave full attention to delineating the activities and behaviors associated with American women's traditional roles. Sweethearts, wives, mothers, and daughters were usually members of the supporting cast, and the cameras seldom followed them into their private domains. Although the rhetoric in combat films consistently proclaimed the importance of women's spheres (politicians, ministers, officers, and enlisted men explained America's commitment and their own allegiance to the war effort in terms of home and motherhood as often as democracy or freedom), the visual record of women's culture is spotty in the best-sellers of the war years, and the attributes connected with female roles in the public mind must be inferred frequently from secondary characters in war films.[1]

Happily, there was one exception to this pattern. *Since You Went Away*, David O. Selznick's 1944 ode to the home front, offered a clearly-drawn wife and mother figure as well as two daughters, one of "sweetheart age," the other an adolescent who missed her father intensely since she was too young for boys. In the film, Anne Hilton's husband had enlisted in the navy and never appeared as a live presence on the screen. Although pictures of Tim Hilton stressed his family's attachment to him, Anne and her two daughters faced the crises of wartime on their own. In the course of the movie they adjusted to war conditions by taking in a boarder to help with their budget, by raising a victory garden, by participating in various volunteer activities, by working—eventually—in the wartime marketplace, and by finding the resources to deal with separation and death in their family circle.

According to his *Memos*, Selznick's ambition in this top-grossing movie was "to tell the story of an American family during wartime," and to this end he tampered with Margaret Wilder's original *Ladies' Home Journal* story, making "the family somewhat more average middle class than is the case in the book" and the problems of the wife and children "as representative of those of the average family as possible." The Hiltons' style of life (a maid, a lovely, rambling home, modern furniture, chic

clothes in general, and a fur coat for Anne) raises some questions about
the middle-class status ascribed to the family. However, as James Agee
noted, "If the Home [in *Since You Went Away*] is not an average U.S.
reality, it is an average U.S. dream."[2]

Agee further suggested that the characterizations in the Selznick
film (directed by John Cromwell) were "authentic to a degree seldom
achieved in Hollywood." The portraits of the wife-mother, the teenage
sweetheart, the adolescent daughter, the forceful black housekeeper, and
the loyal, bachelor friend, were all-American ideals, ones which Americans treasured. *Since You Went Away* was a sure-fire best-seller, the critic
for *Time* and *The Nation* noted, because it "earnestly tackled" an institution and people "disarmingly" loved by Americans.[3]

As Agee hinted, the characterizations in Selznick's movie were at
times overwhelmingly sentimental and idealistic. Nevertheless, the qualities illustrated by the women characters in this top-grossing film were
instructive. Scriptwriter-producer Selznick's characters encapsulated the
most prized attributes of women's traditional roles according to the folklore of the time. The manner in which the female Hilton clan conducted
itself suggested the pattern that most Americans considered desirable and
proper during World War II.

Since You Went Away (Selznick International, 1944)

The first scenes of *Since You Went Away* shift the viewer from a mood of
security to one of loneliness and foreboding. In the opening footage, logs
are seen crackling in the fireplace of a cozy home. As the film credits
begin to run, the audience is thrust suddenly outside the snug home,
seeing it from a distant perspective, fogged by a driving rainstorm that
seems to threaten the house and its surrounding environs. When the
credits end their run, the camera focuses on a leafless tree in the front
yard of the home, showing its branches twisting wildly as it tries to with-
stand the pressures of the wind and rain. The visual message of these
beginning scenes of *Since You Went Away* is fairly obvious. The suburban,
brick home which "seven out of ten Americans would sell their souls
for" is under attack by a violent, unreasonable force. In case any viewer
missed the visual cues or felt overly frightened by the ferocity of the
storm, a reassuring written message quickly appears on the screen, accompanied by the music of "Home, Sweet Home" on the soundtrack.
"This is the story of the Unconquerable Fortress: The American Home
. . . 1943," the audience reads.[4]

Selznick's opening tribute to an "unconquerable American fortress"
establishes the tone that dominates the movie. While war poses a threat

to the home, demanding resiliency and patriotic sacrifices of family members, the film intimates that there is no genuine question about the institution's ultimate survival. The reasons for the durability of the home are shown to lie with all Americans' commitment to it, but women are shown to be the special caretakers of the institution in time of war, and they are further portrayed as conscious of their responsibility and happy about it. For almost three hours, the patrons who made a best-seller of *Since You Went Away* watched a housewife heroine adroitly surmount the trials that war imposes on her home and family. Anne Hilton's resources for this primarily "unpleasant task" come from her devotion to her life as a wife and mother. She expresses no discontent with her roles at any point in the film.

Anne's satisfied attitude toward her lifestyle—and the manner in which she protects her home and family in time of war—offer important evidence to the historian of women's culture. According to Selznick's film, the wife-mother figure is a key person on the home front. Anne Hilton embodied the characteristics that Americans found acceptable in a "housewife heroine," suggesting the behavior, obligations, and rewards that Americans attached to this role reserved for women.

The beleaguered home depicted in the first frames of *Since You Went Away* becomes more personal when the movie introduces the family who lives there in 1943. Abandoning the storm-tossed tree, the film moves viewers slowly into the home through a window on which a service star is prominently displayed. Once inside the home, the camera carefully guides movie-goers through the Hilton's family room, lingering first on the War Department telegram that had disrupted the family by taking breadwinner, Tim Hilton, to the navy, and then swiftly panning the mementos of a couple's life together—a mounted fish caught on Anne's and Tim's honeymoon, bronzed baby shoes, a picture of Anne and the Hilton daughters, Jane and Bridgett, and an overweight bulldog who lies dejectedly before a vacant leather chair. These moments of eavesdropping on the private domains of the Hilton family convey several notions to the movie-going public. The finicky attention to mementos creates an impression of a happy, thriving family, while the war orders, empty chair, and despondent bulldog visually suggest the intrusion of war. The eavesdropping scene generates feelings of interest and concern for the people in the "genteel home in the Middle West," preparing the audience to meet them sympathetically and to take their problems seriously.[5]

Anne Hilton (Claudette Colbert), an attractive, smartly dressed brunette, is the first of the Hiltons to enter the "livable two story seven-room American home" that Selznick had built to capture the idea of home in

the American mind. Anne's return to her "fortress" is not a happy occasion. She has just waved the obligatory, cheerful good-bye to her navy
husband, and closing her front door no longer protects her from "the
storm" outside. "This is the moment I've dreaded," the audience hears
her think as she gazes morosely at a picture of Tim on the hall table,
"coming back to our home alone." Despondently making her way up the
stairs, Anne continues her private talk to Tim (and the audience). "I still
don't know why you should risk your life; you, the best natured and
dearest person in the world. I'll try to remember what you said last night:
that years from now this will seem the greatest adventure we ever had—
even though we had it separately. But I have no courage, I have no
vision, and already I am so very alone."

Anne Hilton's soliloquy suggests the despair that wives were thought
to suffer whenever they were thrust into the head of household position.
Their fears were seen to come from various sources: their prior dependency on their husbands, their reluctance to be alone, their apprehension
about their children, and their lack of an intellectual understanding of the
war effort. In the beginning segments of *Since You Went Away*, Anne
shows no awareness of the reasons for the United States' involvement in
the war. As a wife and mother, she has been sheltered from such matters,
restricting her interests to her home, her family, and her community's
church and social affairs. In the crisis generated by her husband's departure, Anne finds herself with few resources. Reaching the safety of the
bedroom she shared with Tim, Anne clutches his discarded bathrobe and
succumbs to tears, finding comfort in familiar things.

Significantly, in this early moment of weakness and sorrow, Anne
expresses no anger or resentment, even though her husband, who is past
draft age, has volunteered his services to the U.S. Navy. As a helpmate
and mother, the film implies, Anne's function is to accept and support
Tim's decision, assume new household responsibilities cheerfully (if timorously), and maintain a stoic demeanor before her children. Anne begins to adjust to these demands the instant she hears Bridgett (Shirley
Temple) and Jane (Jennifer Jones) burst through the front door, eagerly
yelling, "Mother, where are you?" Swiftly composing herself, she greets
them with an appearance of confidence and geniality, thrusting her own
feelings into the background in order to comfort them. As life on the
home front continues in *Since You Went Away*, Anne carries on as a
"successful wife and mother, tremulous at first but steadying as she
achieves enlarged understanding."[6]

Anne's first major decisions on her own are financial ones. As an
advertising executive, Tim Hilton provided considerably more income
than the U.S. Navy is willing to pay a captain. To make ends meet Anne

rents her lovely bedroom (complete with french windows and a fireplace) to an irascible retired army colonel, William T. Smollett (Monty Woolley). Anne's choice of the colonel as the family boarder is an example of the behavior considered acceptable for women making financial decisions in wartime households. The film suggests that moral and status considerations are as important as additional income. For example, as a navy captain's wife, Anne does not consider renting a room to any serviceman other than an officer. The advertisement she prepares with her daughters' help is specific in that regard. Moreover, a crotchety old man is preferable to the attractive young officer who shows an immediate interest in pretty Jane (soon to celebrate her 16th birthday). Anne's quick refusal to the handsome young man stresses her competency in the role of moral guardian; she will allow no tempting situations in her home.

The connection between financial and moral judgments is accentuated further when Anne is required to make her second major money decision. Faced with a budget deficit, she sorrowfully tells Fidelia (Hattie McDaniel), the Hilton's black live-in domestic, that the family can no longer afford her services. But, she assures Fidelia, after the two women have discussed the war jobs available to the former maid, there will always be a room available for her in the Hilton home. When Fidelia chooses to return to her old room—as an employed worker in a war plant who is tired of the "trashy people" she encounters in boarding houses—Anne refuses her offer of payment for room and board. "That room was always yours and it always will be," she tells Hattie, further insisting that the family would benefit by Hattie's presence. "Mrs. Hilton," Fidelia replies tearfully, "that the most beautiful thing I heard anyone say in my borned days."

While Anne's actions in this scene are clearly patronizing and Fidelia's behavior that of a childlike, dependent black whose primary desire is to be loved by whites, as the film proceeds Fidelia has some moments in which her influence in the family is apparent. As surely as Anne guards the virtue of her daughters, Fidelia watches over the behavior of their mother. She scolds Anne for allowing Jane and Bridgett to see a humorous pin-up recruiting poster of herself drawn by a family friend, Navy Lieutenant Commander Tony Willett (Joseph Cotton), and Fidelia generally views bachelor Tony's visits to the Hilton home with suspicion and censure.

Fidelia's chastisements are presented mainly as a type of comic relief, for she behaves mostly in stereotypical "Mammy" fashion. Yet Anne turns to her for support in times of crisis, Tony courts her favor, the absent Captain Hilton entrusts her with secret gifts for his family and Jane and Bridgett are shown interacting with her in affectionate ways.

The overall impression of Fidelia is that she is a devoted and accepted member of the family group who has no other ambitions for herself. While this portrait undoubtedly does an injustice to authentic black history, it speaks more truthfully about the attitudes of the white community in wartime America. Despite the Office of War Information's suggestion (through the Bureau of Motion Pictures) that Hollywood producers would better contribute to home front morale by not casting "Negroes always in menial or comic parts," *Since You Went Away* presents its only black character in precisely this mode, prompting the conclusion that white Americans' attitudes had budged little since *Gone With The Wind*, in spite of the world conflict and the militancy growing in the black community in the United States.[7]

Anne Hilton's decisions to do her own homemaking chores and to accept a boarder into her roomy, comfortable house are depicted as major changes in Selznick's film. In comparison to the demands which the war imposed on many Americans, these seem minor sacrifices. Historians record that the workers who flooded the cities where defense plants were located lived in garages, basements, tents, refrigerator lockers, and automobiles, while women following their service husbands to rural army camps were often forced to pay up to $50.00 a month to shelter their children in converted chicken coops and dilapidated barns. Within the context of the film, however, Anne's efforts appear credible and praiseworthy—primarily through the introduction of a villain, Emily Hawkins (Agnes Moorehead), who constantly scolds Anne for behaving in ways unsuitable to "our class of people."[8]

Emily, a "venal, hoarding divorcee," is first presented as a shrill voice chiding Anne for her demure, unaggressive behavior when the two women meet in a crowded bar for a cocktail. Shouting to the embarrassed Anne that it is nonsense to be so old fashioned, Emily shoves her way to the bar, finally procuring space for both women. In the ensuing conversation, Emily (whose eyes roam constantly in search of attractive men) reacts in a horrified manner when Anne mentions the boarder in her home. Totally unsympathetic to the war effort, Emily insists that Tim Hilton's first loyalty should be to Anne and the Hilton daughters. Sniffing arrogantly, Emily attacks Tim's choice to enter the navy and Anne's willing adjustment to her new situation. "He is just one of those irresponsible forty-year-old fathers [who dashed] off into uniform," she accuses. Anne disagrees calmly, explaining "He was just miserable being out of it."[9]

Anne's passive demeanor and loyal remarks are given the stamp of male approval when Lieutenant Commander Tony Willett appears suddenly in the cocktail lounge. When the handsome navy officer joins the two women at the bar, Emily openly demonstrates her interest in him, complimenting him and hinting at her availability. Tony's response to Emily is entirely negative, however. He gives his total attention to Anne, ignoring Emily or replying to her questions brusquely. Although Anne later reprimands him for his rude behavior, she allows him to whisk her off to dinner, leaving Emily on her own.

In her other brief appearances in the film, Emily continues as Anne's counterpart. She stockpiles foods, buys new clothes (and makes pointed remarks about her friends' old ones), indulges herself freely on the black market, and disapproves Anne's, Jane's, and Bridgett's involvement in the war effort as unseemly for people of their standing. Emily's unpatriotic attitudes are shown to stem from both her wealth and her position as a woman alone. Neither circumstance appears to strengthen her ability to understand or care for others. On the contrary, according to *Since You Went Away*, Emily's lack of family ties and her economic independence make her a thoughtless, embittered woman, unable to relate to the needs of the larger community. This unattractive portrait of a divorced, well-to-do, assertive woman displayed wartime Americans' antipathy toward females in this category. *Since You Went Away* suggested that they were obstructive, useless persons in a nation at war. Anne offers the final moral judgment on Emily toward the end of the movie. In her only show of temper in the two-hour, 50-minute film, Anne quarrels heatedly with Emily, welcoming her release from a friendship of which she is ashamed when Emily huffily leaves the Hilton home.

Emily is obviously a character of contrast in *Since You Went Away*. Sour-faced, discontent, and critical, she contributes to the war effort only to advance her own interests (Emily is shown organizing USO dances to bring herself into contact with available men). On the other hand, the housewife-heroine in Selznick's top-grossing movie, Anne Hilton, exhibits the opposite qualities of self-sacrifice, compassion, and restraint in unlimited measure. Tony's brief visits as a house guest furnish the milieu for one of the tests of these qualities.

After leaving the bar, Tony and Anne are shown chatting pleasurably over a dinner of wartime steak (hash) and coffee. When Anne learns that Tony has a leave of several days' duration, she immediately invites him to share their home, even though this means further cramping their lifestyle. While Anne moves in with her daughters—who are delighted to see "Uncle Tony" and to share their bedroom with their mother—Colonel Smollett and Fidelia regard "newcomer" Tony with suspicion. Their lack of receptivity toward the charming naval officer establishes the threat he poses in the public's mind. Tony's presence in the household tests Anne's commitment to Tim—for Tony had been a suitor in earlier years and he continues to insist that Anne is his "favorite girl" even while he speaks loyally of Tim.

Despite the tension occasioned by Tony's visit, the ultimate message in this film episode is a heartening one for female/male relationships during war. Ignoring or placating the other adults in her household, Anne encourages Tony's relationship with her children. When Bridgett feels comfortable crawling into Tony's lap, Anne acknowledges her affection, and when Jane develops an intense "crush" on Tony, Anne allows it "to run its course" in an aware and unobtrusive manner. Anne also handles Tony's feelings for herself with ease. In the most overtly sexual scene between Anne and Tony (a moonlit "cigarette stop" while driving home from a USO dance), Tony gazes longingly at Anne and wishes that he could be a "good, heavy, synthetic rubber heel." Anne deftly sidesteps his invitation to marital infidelity by assuring Tony that such behavior "would be synthetic." Tony swiftly agrees, and both appear content with their interchange as they continue homeward.

Censorship codes severely restricted sexual activities in the movies of this era. A passionate kiss between a man and a woman was filmland's most explicit depiction of sexual urges. Sometimes the kiss would be followed by a slow fade-out, a device which encouraged the viewer to use his or her imagination. In *Since You Went Away*, Jane and her soldier-fiance are allowed such a romantic interlude the afternoon of his departure for the European war front. In contrast, Anne and Tony resort to the conventional handshake when he leaves for active duty, solidifying the impression that their friendship poses no threat to Anne's marriage. The constant allusions to Tony's playboy reputation throughout the film heighten the sense that Anne is being tested anytime her persistent premarital flame appears on the home front. On the first of Tony's visits, Anne remains immune to his charms, graciously welcoming him into the Hilton home, and calmly establishing the lines of proper behavior. The propriety of Anne's moral codes is acknowledged by Tony's reactions. He both complies with her softly-worded requests and he continues to speak of Anne as his ideal woman.

After Tony's departure, the Hilton family settles into its wartime routine. While Jane and Bridgett go to school, roll bandages, collect salvage, and sell war stamps, Fidelia continues to work in a war plant, the colonel performs vague services for the army, and Anne struggles to keep her household running on ration points. Having survived both financial crises and a temptation to marital infidelity, the housewife-heroine of *Since You Went Away* next encounters problems arising from her position as a single parent. As Jane prepares to graduate from high school, Anne discovers that Jane's ideas about her future conflict with those that she and Tim had carefully planned.

Recovering from her adolescent crush on "Uncle Tony," Jane has begun to date Colonel Smollett's grandson, Bill (Robert Walker), partly because the gawky soldier seems totally captivated by her, and partly because her compassion is stirred by the colonel's frosty reception of Bill when he drops by the Hilton home for a visit. After an evening of bowling, when the two young people have seated themselves on Jane's comfortable porch, Bill tells her the reasons for the colonel's disdain of him. His family prides itself on the military men in its lineage, he explains—through the rolls of army officers, the Smolletts can trace their ancestry back as far as the American Revolution—but he has been kicked out of West Point, discrediting his family. He deserves his grandfather's censure, Bill says, for he was a failure and has disappointed the colonel greatly. As early as his 10th birthday he frustrated "the great old man," asking questions about whether people hurt each other in war when the colonel gave him a watch carried by a Smollett at Vicksburg during the Civil War. As the camera dwells on Bill and Jane, establishing a quiet, intimate moment, he confesses that he thinks himself a weak person, for the only reason he is now wearing a uniform is that the United States is "fighting for its life." He can never be a professional in the army like his father and grandfather, he states miserably, because he lacks their strength and aggressiveness. At this point, Jane rushes to Bill's defense, insisting "You're fine and strong, but you're just sensitive, that's all." When Bill timorously asks, "Don't you think I'm a failure?" Jane replies with confidence: "A failure? Just because you're not an officer? . . . You are the boys doing all the fighting!"

Jane's and Bill's relationship in *Since You Went Away* seems built around the equation depicted in the tender porch scene. The young soldier, introverted by feelings of guilt and inadequacy, draws confidence from Jane, who is consistently supportive, understanding, and cheerful in his presence. She even determines to speak to the colonel about his treatment of Bill—on her own. Finding the belligerent colonel curt and unreceptive, she turns to her mother for guidance and comfort. Although Anne is disturbed to find her daughter in a serious involvement with an enlisted man who would soon be shipped overseas, she listens to Jane attentively and offers soothing words. While Anne takes no immediate action after Jane's revelations, the concerned expression on her face and the determined squaring of her shoulders informs the audience that she has decided to mediate the situation between Bill and his grandfather. Since her daughter is now involved, Anne's careful dictum to not interfere in the life of her boarder is replaced by a more important priority. As

the family caretaker of proper behavior, Anne needs to shield her daughter
from careless actions. Her resources for accomplishing this lie with her
ability to establish harmony among all parties.

While Anne thinks about the best course to follow to help Jane in
her romantic involvement, Jane's graduation furnishes a different problem
for the housewife-mother. Imbued with a need to be involved, Jane asks
her mother's permission to get a war job. Horrified, Anne responds, "You
certainly may not! You are going to college! . . . I promised your father
and I promised myself that all the things we planned for you are going to
come true, war or no war!" Stressing the importance of Jane's cooperation in her parents' blueprint for her future, Anne remarks, "This is
what your father is fighting for!"

Anne discovers, however, that the impact of war—even on a sheltered home front—cannot be dismissed so easily. The world conflict has
been the preponderant influence in the lives of the young people of Jane's
generation, marking them with a sense of life's fragility. When Jane and
Bill are bowling, they are surrounded by young soldiers who wear their
uniforms with conspicuous swagger but who also confess their homesick-
ness and loneliness at the slightest friendly overture. For Anne's elder
daughter, her parents' careful plans for her future make no sense. Bill
cannot court her leisurely, waiting until she finishes her education and he
is settled in a job to ask for a commitment. And college itself seems silly,
Jane tells Bill as they walk home from her graduation exercise (a somber
ceremony dominated by patriotic symbols and speeches). The new graduate would much prefer to join the WAVES or enter nurses' training so
that she can "really feel like a part of the war effort," Jane confides to
her boyfriend.

As *Since You Went Away* continues its portrait "of what war meant
to the women who stayed at home," Anne Hilton is shown changing her
ideas about Jane as she achieves an enlarged understanding of the sacrifices demanded by war. Anne's new awareness comes from an awakening realization that she is definitely on her own for the war's duration.
Rushing by train to meet Tim Hilton for a hasty good-bye before his
shipment overseas, Anne, Jane, and Bridgett arrive at the overcrowded
hotel designated by Tim too late to see him (their train had been side-
tracked and delayed by priority ones carrying troops). In one of the film's
most poignant scenes, Anne and her daughters, exhausted by the long
trip, huddled together in the packed lobby of the hotel, frantically search
the crowd for Tim Hilton. Finally they hear a page calling their name and
they excitedly push their way to the desk—only to discover that Tim has
already left, barely managing to scribble a note before his departure.
Their weariness and disappointment apparent, the dejected trio find that

there are no available rooms in any hotel in the city and that they are lucky to find spaces, even in the aisles, of a train returning to their home-town. Weathering this situation with her usual fortitude, Anne nonetheless listens with new attention when an elderly woman on the train mentions, with great pride, that her granddaughter is one of the nurses on Corregidor.[10]

The abortive train trip, which *Life Magazine* described as "the most realistic scene in the film," changes Anne's view of the war. Her forced mingling with swarms of displaced Americans and her personal experiences with discomfort and loss in a city transformed by war bring her a new awareness of the impact of the world conflict on the home front. Reevaluating her own sacrifices, Anne becomes more flexible toward her daughter's wishes, agreeing to let Jane train as a Red Cross nurse at least for the summer, and encouraging Bill to drop by often.[11]

The summer of 1943 passes quickly for the Hiltons. Bridgett and the colonel cultivate a "victory garden," the latter losing some of his iras-cibility in the warmth of the Hilton household (although he remains stead-fastly unapproachable on the subject of his grandson). Occasionally a letter from Tim reaches his family, and Jane and Bridgett gather around their mother, eager for this bit of communication from their father. Shortly after such a family reading, when the girls have left their mother alone to read her special portions of the letter (Jane and "Brig" retreat to their bedroom where they hug each other and cry, Bridgett exclaiming, "I miss Pop something awful"), the Hiltons receive disastrous news.

It is the afternoon of August 4, 1943, a date to be carved indelibly on the Hiltons' consciousness. Anne, deep in an afternoon sleep, smiles and dreamily murmurs, "Tim," as Fidelia, home early, walks through the shadowed house with a telegram in her hand. Reluctantly awakening Anne, Fidelia tries to prepare her for awful news, but—as this scene in *Since You Went Away* intimates—there can be no preparation for such a terrible blow. As Anne grabs the telegram, fearfully ripping it open, the camera follows her eyes to the phrase "Missing In Action." Unable to accept this grim information, Anne collapses in a faint in Fidelia's arms, emerging from shock only when she thinks of her children.

The Hilton family's reactions to the War Department's telegram naming Tim among those "Missing In Action" reveal the behavior con-sidered acceptable for bereaved families in time of war. After her initial response of shock and collapse, Anne reasserts her optimism, insisting that none of the family must give up hope. Her daughters agree, saving their tears and prayers for quiet moments in the privacy of their bedroom (Jane gently cautioning Bridgett to "not let mother hear you cry"). Anne also sheds her tears alone. Sitting in Tim's leather chair, clinging simultaneously to a photograph album and the Hiltons' bulldog, Soda, Anne sobs, "He'll come back to us."

Anne's belief in Tim's eventual return and her fervent desire that her daughters share her feelings are shown to be suitable reactions to the War Department's description of Tim's status. In fact, the propriety of Anne's stubborn hope and faithfulness constitutes the major theme in the remaining portions of *Since You Went Away*.

In the development of this theme, the movie first distinguishes between the proper and improper times for families to continue to hope for a serviceman's safe return. In Selznick's film, the message is conveyed to viewers through the motion picture's attention to the young lovers, Jane and Bill.

The couple's casual friendship has ripened into an affectionate, steady commitment by the time Bill receives orders for his shipment overseas. During the soldier's last hours, before joining his troop to board a train for the coast, Jane and Bill walk in the country, happily singing "My Darling Clementine," tumbling in haystacks, and eventually embracing passionately (the kiss followed by a fade-out) in an old barn which has provided them shelter from a sudden rainstorm. While the two are frolicking in the country, Anne determinedly confronts Colonel Smollett, insisting sharply that he has no right to deny his grandson approval and love—especially now, when Bill needs to feel confident and strong. Reluctantly, the colonel admits that Anne is right. He has been very impressed, the crusty old man says, by Anne's capacity to show fortitude when she could have yielded to feelings of anger and hopelessness. The least he can do, the colonel supposes, is give his grandson a proper sendoff. Although pleased by Colonel Smollett's decision, Anne gives herself little credit; her audacious interfering may have come too late, she worries.

As usual in *Since You Went Away*, the housewife-heroine's instincts prove to be correct. While Jane shares Bill's last moments in the train station, the two agreeing to a future marriage and exchanging their most prized possessions (Jane gives Bill her class ring; Bill insists that she take his heirloom watch), the colonel arrives seconds after the troop train has left. Chagrined by his failure to offer his grandson an acceptable farewell, the colonel tries to comfort Jane, and as the movie proceeds, she becomes the substitute recipient for the affectionate feeling he has denied Bill.

In the next segment of *Since You Went Away*, the movie emphasizes that the young boys doing all the fighting are also the ones who die in combat. On a lovely fall day in 1943, Jane, now a grown-up nurse's aide who has abandoned her college plans with her mother's approval, accidentally meets Bridgett when she is wheeling home from school. As the two sisters walk toward their house, Bridgett pushing her bike to enjoy this moment of closeness with her big sister, Jane talks of her plans for the future. Marrying Bill is most important, she explains to "Brig," but she also wants to go to college when the war is over. Teasing each other and laughing, the two girls enter their home, but their mood changes abruptly when they see their mother's face. Another War Department telegram has come to the Hilton home, one which "regrets to inform his family" of the death of William Smollett II at the beachhead of Salerno. When Jane tries desperately to reject the news, insisting that the military has made a mistake, Anne says flatly, "No. You mustn't fool yourself. That would be the worst thing of all. . . . It said he died in action at Salerno." As Jane absorbs her mother's authoritative words, she begins to sob convulsively. "I've known all along," she cries. Pale and quiet, Anne draws Jane into her arms, encouraging her to vent her feelings and to accept Bill's death.

Anne's insistence that Jane abandon hope for Bill's return appears based on her total trust in the accuracy of War Department information. The episode suggests that Americans on the home front placed complete faith in the communications they received from the armed forces. Since neither army nor navy intelligence makes mistakes, according to the film, the Hiltons can continue to believe that Tim is alive (if temporarily unaccounted for), but a telegram that explicitly speaks of death requires a direct confrontation with the loss of a loved one. As the Hiltons and Colonel Smollett begin a mourning period for Bill, *Since You Went Away* reflects the pattern of ordinary American thinking on the subjects of "the sorrow of death and the comfort of religion with an amazing fidelity." The Hilton household is shown to draw comfort from their minister's inspirational sermons, from the affection and support of townspeople at church services, and from private prayers in their moments alone. Solace also comes from memories of happy times and from the conviction that the war is absolutely necessary for Americans "to preserve their sacred heritage of liberty." Losing oneself in work is depicted as an important antidote to grief. Jane follows this course, accepting a position as a nurse's aide in a Rehabilitation Hospital and devoting all her energy and time to soldiers who have been maimed or shell-shocked.[12]

While the Hiltons accept Bill's death with magnanimity, they bolster each other's faith that Tim is alive. Since they cannot send letters to the missing husband-father, Anne begins a journal for Tim, reporting the events of their days so that he can share them later. Anne's nightly sessions at her desk are not presented as unreasonable or pathetic times; indeed her calm assurance that Tim will read her journal one day is depicted as proper wifely behavior.

And it is in this same context that Anne's final sacrifice for the war effort occurs. When Tony once again drops in on the Hiltons during a brief leave, Anne confesses to him that she considers herself a frivolous person who has been denying the obligations imposed by war. "I have a husband who went off to fight for this home and for me," Anne explains, "and I have children . . . [who have shown] courage and intelligence while their mother lived in a dream world. Well, believe me, I've come out of it . . . I want to do something [more]." Although Tony offers Anne swift reassurance, complimenting her effusively for all she has done and remarking that the defense of motherhood and home is the real reason he has joined up (more important, in fact, than Roosevelt's "Four Freedoms"), Anne is not swayed. Although she is worried about her competency, Anne determines that she will do more. She will seek a war job.

The next scenes of *Since You Went Away* follow the housewife-heroine through her experiences as a welder in a shipyard. The screen portraits of women on the job are dramatic ones. The work is depicted as important, dangerous, exhausting, and dirty (Selznick hired Josephine Von Miklo, author of "I Took A War Job," to supervise the technical details of work in a factory). In spite of the grueling demands of a blue collar job, Anne writes Tim (in her journal) that she loves it and feels great admiration for her immigrant coworkers. "Tremendous changes have taken place in the pampered woman who was your wife," Anne reports proudly.

The appropriateness of Anne's decision to make the ultimate sacrifice and enter the marketplace is emphasized by her family's, Tony's and a new worker-friend's approval. The latter, an Eastern European immigrant woman who escaped the Nazis (and a person, Anne writes to Tim, "whose name would not be heard at our country club") wistfully tells Anne, during a coffee break at the factory, that she is "what I thought America was." And Tony affirms not only the housewife-heroine's willingness to get a war job, but her entire conduct through the war (especially Anne's loyalty to Tim) when he once again describes her as his ideal woman in one of the last scenes of the movie.

Tony's laudatory comments occur during a Christmas Eve party at the Hiltons. While neighborhood children carol outside and Fidelia stands grinning in the doorway, Bridgett appears in high heels and "Janie" (as the colonel now calls her affectionately) descends the stairs on the arm of Bill's greatly-mellowed grandfather. When other friends informally join the Hiltons, Anne is a gracious, receptive hostess, welcoming everyone and insisting that the war be put aside for this one evening.

After the festivities, while the house quiets into sleep, Anne sits alone by the Christmas tree, deep in thought. Her casual glance toward the presents under the tree suddenly brings her to full attention. New gifts have been placed among her meager offerings to her children and household—and they all bear a tag from Tim. As Anne picks up the present addressed to her, Fidelia appears in the doorway, crying softly. Mr. Hilton, she explains, entrusted her to deliver his Christmas presents way last summer, and she feels so bad that she has not sent him one in return as the rest of the family has done, in spite of his "Missing In Action" status. In the final confirmation of Anne's stance, pessimistic Fidelia claims that it is she who has not been "on the right side of the Lord." Anne's confidence has convinced her that Mr. Hilton will return, Fidelia affirms, and she wishes that "God would bless Anne" for being so brave and strong.

In Selznick's film, Anne is blessed and her wartime conduct validated. Opening her present from Tim, she sees an exquisite music box which plays their song, "Together." Gazing into space, her face mirroring her nostalgic thoughts as she listens to the tune, Anne vaguely hears the telephone ring. Absently picking up the receiver, Anne's demeanor changes swiftly. As "Oh Come All Ye Faithful" begins to play in the background, the heroine of *Since You Went Away* dashes to tell her children of their "Christmas miracle." Tim not only is alive—he is on the phone and will be coming home to them soon.

In May of 1943, Maurice Revnes, a Metro-Goldwyn-Mayer executive, wrote to Nelson Poynter, Hollywood director of the Bureau of Motion Pictures, Office of War Information, about the OWI's plans for a "Women at Work" month. Revnes was concerned that the OWI's campaign might emphasize women in the marketplace exclusively—ignoring the person who was, "the backbone of the home front, namely, the wife," whom the executive claimed, had been quite neglected. Revnes mentioned that one of his writers was "working on a script, entitled W-I-V-E-S, which would "glorify the wife in the war effort and . . . show how the average wife can employ short cuts in her daily work, take care of her home, children, and still have time for patriotic effort."[13]

The fate of writer Pete Smith's script is not known, but David Selznick's *Since You Went Away* certainly tried to eliminate the lack of attention to wives mentioned by Revnes. Although Anne Hilton's characterization presented a glorified image of the American housewife-heroine—in much the same manner as marines on Guadalcanal were "perfect" soldiers—her portrait revealed the strong attachment Americans felt toward the roles she symbolized. Moreover, *Since You Went Away* provided future generations with a fairly specific description of the expectations associated with those roles.

Foremost, wives were shown to be contented with their societal position. While Anne was depicted as a resourceful and competent person on her own, *Since You Went Away* strongly conveyed the message that this situation was not of her choosing. Her willingness to undertake the decision-making functions in her family emanated from her desire to keep her home intact while her husband enacted his patriotic duty. The happy ending in the film suggested that the Hiltons' post-war life would be affected little by their separate experiences during the world conflict.

The manner in which Anne entered the marketplace, becoming a welder only as a final sacrifice to the war effort, offered a significant comment on Americans' attitudes during the war. The home, Selznick's film proclaimed, was the basic American fortress—a place of safety, comfort, and protection, where family members could be themselves without fear of judgment. And in *Since You Went Away*, Anne Hilton was shown to be the caretaker of that institution, the person who established an environment of caring and receptivity. Although her decision to get a war job was presented with sympathy and approval, it also was couched in the language of a sacrifice for the war. The film clearly intimated that Anne would return happily to her full-time duties as a housewife-mother as soon as the Allies won the victory.

Curiously, even from the perspective of the 1970s, the lasting impression of the housewife-heroine in *Since You Went Away* is that of a self-assured and valuable woman. Selznick's top-grossing "most human, factual picture to date" illuminated the respect and confidence that Americans placed in the women who maintained their favored institutions while men were away.[14]

Americans' willingness to buy tickets in order to follow life on the home front did not preclude, however, their enthusiasm for other types of heroines, as the next chapter demonstrates.

Heroines in Military Life

On May 16, 1943, the first anniversary of the Women's Army Auxiliary Corps, President Franklin D. Roosevelt issued a statement of congratulations and gratitude to the WAACs for their "fine achievements during their first year of service." "One year ago today," the president's message read, "a new page was written into the military history of our nation." American women "were given an opportunity . . . to share with men the greatest privilege of an American citizen—the right to serve in the defense of our country."[1]

Women had not gained the right to participate in the army, navy, and marine corps without controversy. Members of Congress had debated the creation of the women's auxiliary services, one representative insisting that females would be too concerned with "putting on lipstick and looking in mirrors" to accomplish any work. And achieving official rather than auxiliary status took persuasion and time, even after committees formed by the various military branches had recommended that women in the United States be given the same official status enjoyed by women in England and Canada. Despite the praise of the president and the consistent attempts of the Office of War Information to inculcate a positive attitude toward women's direct involvement in military life, negative responses persisted. One marine officer summed up the resistance to women's participation in the military with an emotional curse: "Goddamn it all. First they send us dogs. Now it's women."[2]

The American public's attitude toward women in their new role as paid soldiers is difficult to assess. The news media reported the appointment of Major Oveta C. Hobby to her position as first commander of the WAACs in energetic, praiseworthy tones, and newsreels faithfully reported the activities of the WAACs, WAVES, WAFS, and women marines. Similarly, government spokespersons reminded the public of the contributions of women in the armed forces. Writing for *The Reader's Digest* in 1943, Eleanor Roosevelt pointed out that "All of the services feel that the women have taken their training well, and met the requirements of the jobs assigned to them in many cases, with a higher degree of efficiency than the men who held those jobs before. In every case where a woman has taken over, she has freed a man for a job in active service." The first lady particularly noted the valor of army nurses and WACs in overseas service and suggested that the policy of keeping other women soldiers on the home front was caused by "a false kind of chivalry" which the majority of women would happily forego. "Most of us," Mrs. Roosevelt wrote, "would rather share more fully in the experience our men are enduring."[3]

While the message of government officials was clearly persuasive—attempting to sway public opinion toward an acceptance of women in their unprecedented role—the newsreel coverage of women in the military reflected more ambiguity. The manner in which women adjusted to military routine or the work they actually performed received the same kind of attention as the styles of uniforms that had been designed especially for women soldiers. "WAVES GET UNIFORMS" was as newsworthy as "FIRST WAACS READY" for duty, and news commentators eagerly noted that WACs, upon their arrival in England, showed distinctly feminine characteristics. "Like all women," the narrator bubbled, the WACs' first desire was "to make themselves at home."[4]

Movies produced during the war years also suggested a mixed attitude toward the female soldier. While the uniformed woman made her appearance in Hollywood films early in the war, she was cast mostly in comedy or musical bit parts where she served as a vague romantic interest for stars such as Bud Abbott and Lou Costello or where she provided musical entertainment for large gatherings of appreciative draftees. As the war continued, and greater numbers of women entered the armed forces, the pattern shifted somewhat. Women in uniforms were given longer, more substantial parts, and they were sometimes shown performing dangerous work such as nursing in combat zones or piloting supply planes as well as executing supportive duties on the home front.[5]

The trend in Hollywood features of the war years appeared toward a heightened visibility of women in the armed forces. Yet only three best-selling movies of the period featured military heroines as major characters, and of the three—So Proudly We Hail (Paramount, 1943), A Guy Named Joe (MGM-Loews, 1944), and Here Come the WAVES (Paramount, 1945)—only the first attempted to explore, in a serious manner, the impact of war and military routine on the lives of women who joined up to serve their country. MGM-Loews' production, while casting Irene Dunne in the role of a competent and independent aviator, focused more dramatically on the "guy named Joe," the lone-wolf male pilot who had to learn to sacrifice individualism for the more productive wartime values of cooperation and submission to an organized plan. Paramount's Here

Come the WAVES dealt more directly with women's adjustment to military life, allowing Betty Hutton (who played a dual role as twins in the WAVES) to remark about her experience: "I knew things were going to be tough, but I didn't know there were going to be so many laughs either." This positive attitude toward women's involvement in the military permeated the dialogue in the film, but the action in *Here Come the WAVES* revolved around the twins' competition for singer Bing Crosby's affections. The primary message of both *A Guy Named Joe* and *Here Come the WAVES* was that women who became soldiers retained their attachment to women's traditional culture. While the female characters in the films were shown to be capable in the performance of their duties, their motivating concern was to please or capture the men in their lives.[6]

So Proudly We Hail deviated somewhat from this formula. Although the nurses in the movie were shown to be interested in romance, the movie also explored their adjustments to military routine, emphasizing the affection and loyalty that developed in their relationships as well as the tensions and quarrels that occurred among them. Moreover, the film illuminated the importance of the work the nurses performed, highlighting their proficiency, impassivity, and stamina on the combat front. The box-office popularity of *So Proudly We Hail* suggests that Americans were very willing to visualize women as combat heroines—as long as they were performing the work which, according to Eleanor Roosevelt, "has been traditional for women in every war . . . from the days of Florence Nightingale and Clara Barton down to our day."[7]

The widespread public approval accorded the images of women in *So Proudly We Hail* further suggests that, in this instance, analysts in the Domestic Branch of the Bureau of Motion Pictures were more in tune with popular attitudes toward women's role in the war effort than Paramount's scriptwriters. Unlike most of the top-grossing war pictures produced during World War II, the movie's plot and characterizations were directly influenced by recommendations that emanated from this media agency within the Office of War Information. The rarity of this occasion is important to note, for most attempts of the Domestic Bureau of Motion Pictures to alter feature films toward a more "realistic" depiction of the war soured their box-office appeal. The Bureau's chief, Lowell Mellett, warned his Hollywood staff about this sort of tampering in a lengthy letter dated December 30, 1942. Faced with an incipient revolt among the same Hollywood executives who a year earlier had requested a liaison agency with the federal government to help them maximize their war contributions, Mellett took a firm stand about the Bureau's monkeying with Hollywood's creative talent. "I don't think you ever realized how rugged a character I am in that respect," Mellett wrote to Nelson Poynter, the BMP's director in Hollywood:

> You boys and girls have been pretty proud of the job done on PITTS-BURGH and KEEPER OF THE FLAME. I think your pride can only result from the appearance of your own stuff in those two pictures. Catching both of them cold, as I did, I was shocked by the way the machinery creaked. As stories they do not flow with continuity and naturalness; the propaganda sticks out disturbingly . . . PITTSBURGH did not have a successful run at Keith's, business falling off definitely after the first two days; which may or may not have been a partial result of the thing I mention. If the two pictures should prove to be less than successful commercially, it is not unreasonable to expect that we will get the blame and that the disposition to incorporate themes suggested by us will be materially affected.

Mellett feared that poor box-office receipts would cause "the industry to start demanding a sacrificial goat," and he cautioned Poynter, "the goat would not be me, if I can judge by all the nice things they say; it would be the man on the firing line."[8]

Mellett's warning to his Hollywood staff included studio executives' specific complaints—"One thing to which [they] strongly object is very much dealing on our part with writers, directors and others in [their] employment"—as well as their general fear that the Domestic Bureau of Motion Pictures might present "a threat to the freedom of the motion picture industry." Paradoxically, the Domestic Bureau of Motion Pictures survived its crisis with the movie industry only to find a more intractable opponent in the Republican-Conservative Democrats' Congress elected in 1942. When the Office of War Information's budget was reviewed in the summer of 1943, funding for the Domestic Branch of the BMP was sharply curtailed by the conservative coalition determined to eliminate what they called "Roosevelt's Propaganda Machine." Although the Overseas Branch of the BMP maintained an active pace throughout the war, influencing Hollywood's products through its power to deny export approval, the Domestic Branch of the Bureau of Motion Pictures was phased out in the summer of 1943.[9]

The demise of the Domestic Branch of the Bureau of Motion Pictures ended a promising relationship between the Hollywood industry and the staunchly liberal reviewing staff that functioned under Nelson Poynter. Despite their earlier quarrels, *The Hollywood Reporter* lamented the shuttering of the Western BMP office, noting that "It is agreed by most studio creators working with the OWI here that Poynter has done a good job, nobody in the industry has been pushed around, and situations arising over differences of opinion have been tactfully handled."[10]

The short lifespan (and incomplete records) of the Domestic Bureau of Motion Pictures make any generalizations about its impact a tenuous matter. When the Western Office was created in June of 1942, its commission was "to advise the motion picture maker about what is useful for portrayal on the screen from the viewpoint of the war information program." During its limited existence the Hollywood staff worked diligently "to help the industry 'raise its sights.' " The group prepared a *Manual for the Motion Picture Industry* in the summer of 1942 and lengthened it with supplements during its active year of interaction with movie-makers.[11]

The guidelines written by the Hollywood staff of the BMP rank "as probably the most comprehensive statement of OWI's interpretation of the war." Within the *Manual*, World War II was defined as a "people's war"—a struggle against fascism in which every person had a concrete stake. This was particularly true for minorities and women, the *Manual* pointed out. While neither group had achieved a utopia in democratic nations, fascism proscribed any rights they had gained to participation as citizens in society.[12]

The Bureau of Motion Pictures' definition of war goals provided its own framework for criticizing the scripts which Hollywood studios submitted to them. Imbued with a sense of mission, the Bureau staff at times went too far, suggesting dialogue and inserting patriotic speeches that appeared stilted and unnatural to filmmakers interested in profit and accustomed to reading the public mind. On these occasions, studio executives wasted no time. They went over Poynter's head and consulted with his boss in Washington, D.C., Lowell Mellett. This grey-haired, witty, former Scripps-Howard journalist and presidential advisor invariably sided with the movie industry. Although a New Deal liberal committed to the interpretation of World War II expressed in the *Manual for the Motion Picture Industry*, Mellett was uncompromisingly in favor of the freedoms of the First Amendment. In his view, the function of the Bureau of Motion Pictures was solely to suggest general themes or general information to Hollywood's creative talent, who could do with the information whatever they liked.[13]

A case study of *So Proudly We Hail* reveals that, in this particular instance, Paramount executives chose to listen to Bureau analysts and that they eventually profited thereby. Paramount sent writer Allen Scott's draft of the movie script to Nelson Poynter in October of 1942 where it was quickly read by BMP staff members, Dorothy Jones and Marjorie Thorson, the latter submitting a review of the movie script to Poynter on October 19th. The script review followed the general pattern developed by the Bureau of Motion Pictures over time: the grade of the picture was estimated, an "A" designating films of most importance; the movie was classified in terms of its war content, "Major," "Minor," or "Not Related"; a brief synopsis was written; and, finally, the script reviewer assessed the weaknesses and strengths of the film from the framework established earlier by the Office of War Information. Since producer-director Mark Sandrich's film was considered an "A" movie with "Major" war content, it seemed to receive priority attention from the Hollywood BMP staff.[14]

The records of the Bureau show that *So Proudly We Hail* was reviewed three times by different analysts working in Poynter's Hollywood office, twice while the feature was still in script stage, and once as a "release print." No analyst's name appeared on the second review, but both the first and third reviews were written by women, apparently in some collaboration with Dorothy Jones, a staff member who was also beginning her publishing career as "a pioneer in film content analysis."[15]

The first review, written by Marjorie Thorson for inter-office use, described *So Proudly We Hail* as "the story of eight Army nurses who see service on Bataan. Specifically . . . Senior Lieutenant Janet Davidson (the part would eventually be played by Claudette Colbert) who leaves San Francisco with her unit early in December." Continuing her précis, Thorson wrote:

> She and the nurses under her command are bound for Honolulu—but they never get there. Pearl Harbor is bombed while they are still at sea, and the transport ship is ordered to another unknown destination, which proves to be Bataan. On the way the survivors of a torpedoed ship are picked up; one of them is Lt. John Sumners. Between him and Janet there is an instant attraction. Janet fights it, feeling that her whole duty is to the war and the part she must play in it. When she and John are separated on Bataan, and the frightfulness of death is all around her, she begins to feel that she has been wrong to deny the only happiness she may ever live to know. But when she and John meet again just before her unit has to evacuate the base hospital near the front lines, she finds that John has changed. Now it is he who feels the fight is too big and too terrible to allow for personal desires. The pair meet again when both are evacuated to Corregidor. When John volunteers to undertake a mission from which both know he may never return, he and Janet decide to marry. It is against regulations, but they persuade the chaplain to perform the ceremony, and Janet's superior officer, Captain MacGregor, witnesses it. When John goes, Janet promises to be waiting for him at "The Rock" when he returns. However, it becomes evident that the fortress will have to surrender, and the nurses are ordered evacuated. To the end Janet fights against going, pleading that John will expect to find her there. Captain MacGregor is forced to tell her that for a week John has been considered lost. Janet collapses into a kind of coma from which it seems that nothing can rouse her—until, on the boat that is finally taking her back to San Francisco, a young navy doctor pieces together her story from the girls who have served with her. He thinks he knows what her trouble is and how he can remedy it. To the comatose girl

he reads a letter that has come for her from John. In it John tells her not only that he loves her but, through the fighting and suffering he has known, he has begun to see what the war is all about—and the kind of peace he is determined their children shall have. As the doctor reads, the light of intelligence returns to Janet's face. The ship is entering San Francisco harbor as the conviction overcomes her that she and John *will* find each other again.[16]

Thorson's synopsis revealed that Allen Scott's draft was, at this early stage, little more than a routine Hollywood love story conveniently re-worked for a wartime setting. Her comments included several pithy criticisms of Paramount's script—and virtually no praise. "The idea is all right," was the best she could do, "but the accent is all wrong." Script-writer Scott's efforts toward clarifying the issues of the war amounted to "much verbiage and little force." And Thorson particularly disliked the image of women in the military: "The nurses are hysterical; they grow petulant and irritable under strain." While hoping for some opportunity to steer the film into more constructive channels, Thorson also observed that it might be wise to discourage filming of this story at this time.[17]

Although Nelson Poynter would be chastised tactfully by BMP chief, Lowell Mellett, barely two months in the future for interfering with Hollywood's creative talent, his approach to Paramount Studios was a much softer one than Thorson advised. In a letter dated October 26, 1942, Poynter thanked Mark Sandrich "for letting me see the script of SO PROUDLY WE HAIL," praising the film as one "of enormous value to the war information program." The changes he had to suggest were intended "to lift your sights even higher than they are," Poynter wrote, and the introductory paragraph of his letter concluded with an expression of empathy for the difficult task of the producer-director and an offer to meet personally with Sandrich or Scott if either should desire.[18]

The remainder of Poynter's letter addressed the weaknesses that he and his staff had isolated in *So Proudly We Hail*. "An attempt is made," he wrote, "to examine the issues of the war." While this was "most laudable," Poynter wondered if it would be possible "to link the issues" of war more directly to the "personal lives of the characters we come to know." These fictionalized persons seemed to exude a sense of martyrdom, Poynter maintained, a condition which did not "augment audience sympathy." "There is almost a whining quality to their self-pity," the Hollywood chief noted, especially in the speeches that alluded to the mistakes that the American people had made in the past. Poynter asked for at least one character who "could see the positive, affirmative contribution that Bataan offered," and he suggested, as background, that optimism was possible because Americans had assessed their enemy swiftly after Pearl Harbor and Bataan. Credit needed to be given, he remarked, to an isolationist nation that had quickly converted to global commitment before experiencing a disaster such as Dunkirk.[19]

Poynter's letter to Sandrich also expressed concern about the depiction of America's Filipino and Chinese allies in *So Proudly We Hail*, but for the purposes of this work, his interest in the portrait of army nurses is most significant. "Are the nurses presented in such a manner as to inspire the maximum of confidence in them?" he asked:

> In an obvious effort to humanize these girls who are fighting side by side with men in the war, it would seem that some of the worst feminine characteristics have been emphasized. The girls quarrel among themselves; grow irritable and petulant under strain; seize and magnify rumors; often seem more interested in masculine attention than in their work; exhibit very little respect to their superior officers; disobey regulations concerning fraternization with enlisted men.
>
> A certain amount of this sort of thing is all right; but these nurses are entrusted with a deeply serious and responsible job. Nursing units are almost invariably high in morale and discipline.[20]

Poynter's letter was dated October 26, 1942. By November 19th of the same year, the Hollywood BMP had received Allen Scott's complete script and a second response had been written. Noting that the script had been somewhat revised on the basis of Poynter's suggestions, the BMP staff writer observed that the changes made by Sandrich and/or Scott had measurably improved the film from the standpoint of the Office of War Information.[21]

The second version of Paramount's story of army nurses offered a better treatment of the issues of the war. Poynter's proposal that the issues would be more strongly expressed if they were shown to be personally linked to the film characters' lives had been adopted. For example, "John's letter, at the end of the script," the BMP analyst noted, "appears to have been re-edited and brings into much sharper focus what this war means to the people of the story and the people of the world."[22]

Furthermore, the mood of pessimism which had infused Scott's earlier draft had been moderated. While still emphasizing the terrible disaster of Bataan, inspiring historical parallels had been drawn in the script dialogue: "Valley Forge," remarked one of the nurses in version two, "was no strawberry festival either." While still pointing out that Americans were mistaken "for thinking we could ignore the war," Scott's completed script altered the whining tone that Poynter had disliked, substituting characters who conveyed a sense of mission and responsibility: "We have learned the hard way, but we have learned while there is still time," the message ran.[23]

Changes were also observed in *So Proudly We Hail*'s portraits of United States' allies in the Pacific—courageous Filipino characters were added and the use of the derogatory term "Chinaman" was deleted. And the depiction of army nurses was more satisfying to BMP analysts:

> The nurses, particularly in the latter part of the story, are more constructively presented. They work hard because they feel it means something, not because they are hopeless martyrs to a cause they do not understand. In the early portions of the story they remain a rather unpleasant crew, but the curse is taken off their petty feuds and rumor-mongering by their devotion to their work in the last part of the script. They are still human—sometimes all too human—but they do not whine and they are genuinely likeable.[24]

Although the BMP's November review of *So Proudly We Hail* described Paramount's second version as a "much more effective contribution to the war information program than the first," the Hollywood analysts were not entirely satisfied. The movie script had still not reached its fullest potential, they suggested, particularly since it was "the first film [produced during the war years] to present the work being done by women on an active war front."[25]

The BMP's final review of *So Proudly We Hail* was dated June 24, 1943. One suspects that during this seven-month hiatus in the written record, some type of informal communication occurred between the Western BMP and Paramount Studios. This was, however, the same period in which Hollywood executives were in revolt, and Frank Freeman of Paramount was among those who complained to Lowell Mellett about Poynter's staff tampering with the talent in his employ. Freeman evidently felt that direct contact between Poynter and his directors or scriptwriters was a threat to his control. Mellett told Nelson Poynter, in his letter of December 30, 1942, that while Freeman had no objections to any of his writers or directors contacting the Hollywood BMP on their own initiative, Freeman strongly insisted that "if our office wishes to take up any matters concerning the picture with a writer, director or producer, . . . that this be done through his office. This does not mean, he [Freeman] says, that there may not be all such discussions as are necessary, but that he does desire to know about these discussions." Freeman also singled out some of the BMP's efforts on *So Proudly We Hail* for special criticism. Mellett wrote, "he considers harmful the preparation of suggested dialogue, such as the speech of the army chaplain and the speech of the nurse in . . . *So Proudly We Hail*."[26]

Unfortunately, the dialogue suggestions to which Freeman referred apparently were not kept as a part of the official records of the Hollywood BMP. Perhaps Poynter or members of his staff scribbled patriotic lines on the margins of scripts they read—or superimposed their own words over the dialogue prepared by scriptwriters. In his letter to Poynter in which Mellett explained Freeman's complaints, Mellett placed the offending material in "your letter to Mark Sandrich," but Poynter's letter of October 26, 1942, included no such detailed suggestions.[27]

Whatever the origin of the material to which Freeman objected, his complaints to Lowell Mellett seemingly bore fruit. The Hollywood office of the Bureau of Motion Pictures apparently operated more cautiously during the rest of its brief existence—at least in the case of *So Proudly We Hail*, no written correspondence was recorded between November, 1942, and June, 1943.

The BMP's final review of Paramount's film did reveal a much-changed picture, however. The simple love story transposed to a wartime setting had become a movie which made an "outstanding contribution to the Government's War Information Program." This was particularly true of *So Proudly We Hail*'s depiction of nurses. Peg Fenwick, the Bureau's analyst who wrote the third review, commented: "The picture serves as documented proof that women have an obligation to the war effort equal to that of men and that they are capable of fulfilling that obligation."[28]

Fenwick's synopsis of the release print of *So Proudly We Hail* illustrated the extent to which Paramount had incorporated the war content suggestions of the BMP. New characters whose lives and goals were inextricably linked to the war were added, and much more attention was given to the actual performance of nurses in stressful conditions. Fenwick, herself, appeared enthused about the motion picture, as her synopsis revealed:

> On a ship bound for America in May, 1942—is a small group of nurses—veterans of Bataan. One of their number, Lieutenant "Davey" Davidson (Claudette Colbert) lies on the deck, unseeing, uncaring. The ship's medical officer asks the other nurses to tell him something of their common experiences, in the hope of discovering some clue to her present trance-like condition.
>
> Davey's small unit of nurses shipped out of San Francisco in late November, 1941, on their way to the Philippines. Their ship was part of a large convoy, carrying men and materials to the islands. The news of Pearl Harbor was a bombshell thrown into what had been, till that moment, a carefree voyage, and the nurses were given their first taste of war shortly after when one of the ships in the convoy was torpedoed by a Jap submarine. The survivors were brought to their ship, which was hastily converted into a hospital ward; among them were Lieutenant John Somers (George Reeves), to whom Davey was unwillingly drawn and a young nurse, Olivia Darcey (Veronica Lake), silent and embittered, who angrily turned away from the friendly overtures of her companions.
>
> Davey put Olivia in the same cabin with another nurse, Joan (Paulette Goddard), a gay, flirtatious girl, currently enamoured of "Kansas" (Sonny Tufts), one of the Marines aboard. And one night, when Olivia's sullenness

and rudeness had provoked a fight between herself and Joan, Davey took the girl to task for her behavior and learned that she was brooding over the violent death of her fiance, whom she had seen killed and mutilated by Japanese bullets. Now Olivia lives for the moment when she may find a way to retaliate for her fiance's death.

Landing at Marivales, the nurses were taken to Captain "Ma" McGregor (Mary Servoss), a veteran nurse with a son in service in the Philippines. They were put to work immediately, to relieve other nurses staggering with fatigue because of the increasing load of wounded. Horrified, Davey learned that Olivia had asked for and received duty with wounded prisoners. But when she reached the prisoners' tent, it was to find Olivia in tears, cursing her own inability to sink to the level of barbarism of the enemy.

From the time of their landing, the nurses' life [*sic*] became a nightmare. Wounded arriving constantly, no sleep, dwindling medical supplies, food growing scarcer—and each welcome rumor of help from home proving unfounded. During one of the hasty and periodic retreats, the nurses were able to make their escape only through the sacrifice of Olivia, who went out to meet an incoming Jap task force and destroyed both them and herself with a hand grenade. In the hills, their encampment was mercilessly bombed in spite of the huge Red Cross flag which Davey and the others had so carefully placed in a clearing, and one of their group was killed.

But there were moments of compensation in the midst of the horror. John arrived unexpectedly for a few hours stay-over and Davey realized the futility of fighting any longer against their love. Joan's life was gladdened by frequent visits from "Kansas" who had an engaging way of popping up at intervals. But these respites were short-lived. In spite of the gallant action of American and Filipino units, the enemy pressed closer. And one night, the order came to evacuate to Corregidor. Davey, learning that John had just been brought in wounded, stayed behind after seeing the others off in order to attend an emergency operation on his leg and then helped him into a small rowboat, one of hundreds crossing to the island fortress. Joan took "Kansas" to Corregidor by the simple expedient of knocking him out and dragging him to a boat.

On Corregidor, after a few days' respite, the horror began again . . . repeated bombings echoed down into the tunnels. In spite of the regulation forbidding nurses to marry, Davey and John were wed by the chaplain with "Ma" McGregor's blessing and the following day John left for Mindanao to try to bring back some much-needed quinine. But before his return, Davey's unit was ordered to prepare secretly to leave for Australia. Davey rebelled, wanting to wait until John came back. But her rebellion was short-lived when she learned that he had been officially listed "missing." The shock, coming on top of months of overfatigue, undernourishment, and shattered nerves caused a complete collapse.

Since that moment, she has lain in a coma, unseeing, uncaring. That is the story of Bataan, told by the nurses to the ship's doctor. The doctor knows now that it is fear for John which is chiefly responsible for Davey's present condition. In his pocket he has a letter written to Davey which proves that John has arrived safely in Mindanao. As he reads the letter aloud to the assembled group of nurses, Davey stirs, comes to life. For John's letter is a testament of faith in the cause for which they have all fought—and in the future he hopes to help create—with Davey by his side.[29]

Fenwick's synopsis of the release print of *So Proudly We Hail* ably captured the essence of the film that the movie-going public catapulted into best-seller ranks. By 1943, cinema patrons were apparently ready for a feature picture that focused primarily on women's experiences in combat conditions. Paramount's choice of army nurses to represent women's participation in the overseas war effort proved a popular one—most likely because nurses were the most obvious women to be found in the combat zone during World War II. But also, perhaps, because the profession was widely acknowledged as one traditionally given over to the female half of the American population.[30]

So Proudly We Hail's success at the box-office validated the efforts of Poynter and his Hollywood BMP staff in their attempt to "raise the sights" of movie executives when their films dealt with military heroines. (Subsequent efforts of filmmakers showed a reversion to comedy or secondary parts for female soldiers in top-grossing movies.) Unfortunately, the Western Office of the BMP did not survive long enough to receive acclaim for its work. In retrospect, however, it seems rather clear that this government agency's perception of the image of women at war exerted a powerful magnetism on the American public. The money-paying masses of Americans liked heroines who understood the causes of the war; women who willingly renounced comforts, sleep—even their lives—in their dedication to their work. The inclusion of characters of this dimension in Paramount's film appeared to happen primarily by request of the Bureau of Motion Pictures.[31]

Of course, *So Proudly We Hail* also displayed the essentially conservative attitudes about women that permeated American society even during the war years. While the nurses in the movie were shown performing admirably under duress, the meaning or purpose in their lives came from their liaisons with men—not from an attachment to their work. Olivia Darcey (Veronica Lake) willingly sacrificed herself to save other nurses—but her grudge against the Japanese soldiers whom she stoically marched to encounter (with a grenade tucked in her bosom) came from their bestial killing of her fiance—not the immediate presence and threat of the Japanese to her colleagues. Joan (Paulette Goddard), although a frivolous, cheerful person, was similarly involved with the marine who attracted her. When the evacuating notice came to Marivales, ordering her group to Corregidor, Joan attended first to "Kansas," "knocking him out and dragging him into a boat," and taking him to Corregidor, thus insuring her present commitment and, perhaps, a future one. Lt. Davey Davidson, the star of the film, offered the clearest example of Americans' mixed attitudes toward military heroines. She was a dramatic figure, poised and controlled through much of the movie, and extraordinarily capable in the performance of her duty. Yet she disobeyed military laws regarding marriage and she ended her war experience in an unseeing, uncaring state—which only a letter from her new husband could penetrate.

The popularity of *So Proudly We Hail* suggested that Americans felt most comfortable with an image of the military heroine that reflected a female sturdily committed to traditional ideas about woman's place. Female soldiers were acceptable on the combat front as long as they performed the usual work of women and as long as they still gave first priority to the men whom they loved. No box-office hit of the war years challenged this view; in fact, Paramount's story of army nurses emerged as the only best-selling feature that tried to deal with the female soldier in a serious fashion. And while the American public appeared to like the movie very much, reviewers were lukewarm or openly hostile. "This is probably the most deadly-accurate picture that will ever be made of what war looks like through the lens of a housewives' magazine romance," James Agee remarked in *The Nation*.[32]

Action war pictures remained primarily a male domain during World War II. The drama of marines landing at Guadalcanal or Army Air Force pilots arduously training for hazardous duty in the Pacific or the daring bombing of Tokyo early in the war held first sway over the public mind. Women were not entirely ignored in these films, however. The sweethearts, wives, and mothers of servicemen were shown to be important persons, often exerting, through their support and independence, a major influence on their men's actions. In films of the war years, they also were shown to be military heroines.

Air Force (Warner Brothers, 1943) was one of the most violently masculine combat movies filmed during World War II. Producer-director Howard Hawks' picture told the story of the crew of a B-17 bomber, the *Mary Jane*, one of eight Flying Fortresses that left California on December 6, 1941, embarked on a supposedly routine flight for Hawaii. After hours of uneventful flying, Captain Quincannon (John Ridgely) and his crew were approaching their destination—Hickam Field—when their radio suddenly brought the news of the Japanese attack on Pearl Harbor. Caught off-guard—their plane unarmed and no alternative rendezvous planned—the crew of the *Mary Jane* was required to fend for itself. In the course of the movie, they managed this task well—hop-scotching across the Pacific to Wake Island, Manila, in the Philippines, and eventually Australia. Their emergency, haphazard journey was a costly one, however; Captain Quincannon was killed during a mission to bomb a Japanese convoy bound for the Philippines, and the *Mary Jane* was crippled beyond repair in action off the coast of Australia. Yet the majority of the crew of the Flying Fortress survived to become members of a coordinated military effort. The ending scenes of *Air Force* intimated that the teamwork that had carried the crew of the *Mary Jane* through its early dislocation and alienation was active on a national scale only four months after Pearl Harbor.[33]

A concise summary of Warner Brothers' 1943 movie necessarily excludes women characters. In contrast to the film experiences of the nurses in *So Proudly We Hail*, the crew of the *Mary Jane* encountered no females in their combat experiences. The drama of overseas duty in the Army Air Force, the movie implied, was entirely a masculine experience. Yet women did appear in *Air Force*—and the brief scenes devoted to them suggest the types of behavior that Americans found acceptable for the mothers and wives of servicemen.[34]

The opening episodes of *Air Force* occur in an unnamed airbase in California. Captain Quincannon and his crew of eight have just received orders to leave on a training flight to Hawaii. The men lounge about, talking quietly, their enthusiasm for the mission subdued by their concern about leaving their families. The undertones of anxiety are relieved somewhat when the crew is given permission to call home and say good-bye—although their destination or the length of their mission cannot be revealed.

Only two women are able, on such short notice, to hurry to the base for a personal farewell—the young assistant radioman's mother (Dorothy Peterson) and Captain Quincannon's wife (Ann Doran). Both are determinedly cheerful and stoic. Henry Chester's mother listens calmly to her son's excited prattle, complimenting him for knowing so much when he speaks of his job and sharing his high opinion of the *Mary Jane*'s pilot and the other crew members. Mrs. Chester, in fact, insists on meeting Henry's captain, and she later finds a quiet moment in which to ask him to look after her boy. Captain Quincannon shows no surprise at Mrs. Chester's request, reassuring her by accepting responsibility for Henry's welfare. The final good-bye scene between mother and son is a moving one—there are no tears but Mrs. Chester's lips tremble and the two gaze at each other directly and affectionately—as though trying to memorize each other's face.

The leave-taking between Captain and Mrs. Quincannon conveys a different mood. While Mrs. Chester is a resigned, passive figure—needing assurance that another adult would look after her boy—Mary Quincannon is an ebullient, openly affectionate woman. She arrives on the air base only moments before take-off, delayed by a pesky flat tire. In their brief talk, the Quincannons tease each other about the honeymoon-vacation they have yet to experience, even though they have a son. When the captain is called to his plane, Mary says, still in a bantering tone, "It [our marriage] has been fun—every minute of it. I guess I'm just lucky." "Me, too," Quincannon replies, "So long, kid." As the captain turns to walk toward his plane, the camera stays with Mary, and apprehension appears on her face for the first time. She remains a lonely figure as the Flying Fortress thunders down the runway, a military wife who has given her husband a proper, optimistic send-off and a woman who is now alone, except for her small child.

These brief clips in *Air Force* revealed a pattern of behavior that appeared frequently in best-selling masculine combat pictures. Mothers were grief-stricken but resigned, smothering their fears by taking pleasure in their sons' accomplishments and invariably being reassured about their boys' welfare by compassionate senior officers. "Are you happy?" mothers asked frequently. The inevitable affirmative answer was usually sufficient. Occasionally, as in *This Is the Army* (Warner Brothers, 1943), a mother was shown to be recalcitrant. In the case of Mrs. Nelson, her ambivalence was caused by the loss of one son in combat. In the end, however, Mrs. Nelson realized that her second boy was also needed in the war effort. After months of clinging to Ted, she let him go, explaining, "[The army] is what I raised you for—to be a credit to your country and to yourself. Don't worry any more, son. Just take care of yourself—and give it to them." Judging from these films, Americans' attitudes toward pacifistic mothers were rather harsh during World War II. The proper behavior demanded of women with sons of military age was to send them off gracefully, trusting the officers of the various armed forces to look after the rest of their growing up.

Sweethearts and wives were shown to be equally patriotic and more optimistic. The melancholy overtones of a mother's letting go of her son were not apparent in the relationships of adult women and men. In *Winged Victory*, a 1944 20th Century-Fox box-office success, two wives learned of their husbands' imminent departure for war fronts accidentally at a party (the men had decided to keep their news a secret until the last moment). Neither woman betrayed her knowledge; instead they conspired to maintain a normal facade, calmly planning a picnic for all four of them the next week-end and keeping their worries to themselves. In a later scene in the Army Air Force barracks, about the time that the husbands were telling their wives of their overseas orders, the culprit who had spilled the news offered an evaluation of the wives' behavior: "What a swell bunch of girls," he emoted. "They knew it was the last time they'd see [them] before the big hop, but you'd never guess it. No bawling or nothing, sweet and gay as the devil. Oh, they did a good job those girls."

The type of resolute cheerfulness that the women in *Winged Victory* projected was standard behavior for movie sweethearts and wives when they were required to "say good-bye" to their servicemen. Emotional outbursts, tears or resentments were reserved for later moments alone or with women friends or mothers. Moreover, military wives in the popular war films of the World War II period attempted to shield their husbands from worries about themselves, often keeping their pregnancies secret until their babies arrived for fear of over-burdening their soldier-husbands on combat fronts.

Wives also responded to the maiming of their husbands with fortitude and an acceptance that the sacrifice was unavoidable. In *Thirty Seconds Over Tokyo* (MGM, 1944), Ellen Lawson heard of her husband's loss of his leg from his commander, General Doolittle. She determined to travel to the hospital immediately, although she was in her final months of pregnancy, for Ted Lawson was severely depressed and needed her. She had to convince him, she sobbed to her mother, that the disfigurement was not important, "as if anything would make any difference to me as long as he is alive," she insisted.

In addition to confronting the exigencies of war with forbearance, the wives of servicemen in best-selling combat films also articulated their goals once the war was over. Invariably their dreams centered on having their husbands back, and homes and babies and good peaceful lives. Working in the marketplace was depicted solely as a patriotic effort, necessary because of their men's absences and America's need for full wartime production. Although movie wives spoke of the importance of keeping busy, their options seemed limited to three choices: having a baby or caring for children already born; participating in volunteer war efforts; or working in a defense plant. Few wives or mothers of servicemen were shown attempting all three—with the possible exception of Anne Hilton, whose life on the home front was dramatized solicitously in *Since You Went Away*.[35]

The image of the military heroine who was defined through her relationship to a serviceman was mainly a positive one. The brief footage devoted to women in top-grossing films such as *This Is the Army* (Warner Brothers, 1943), *Air Force* (Warner Brothers, 1943), *Guadalcanal Diary* (20th Century-Fox, 1943), *Thirty Seconds Over Tokyo* (MGM, 1944) or *Winged Victory* (20th Century-Fox, 1944) suggested that the devotion and caring of mothers and wives contributed to soldiers' competency and well-being. Men on the combat front often alluded to the importance of the women in their lives, explaining their involvement in the war in terms of protecting their homes and families. In one of the most poignant scenes in *Guadalcanal Diary*, when a contingent of marines was slaughtered on a lonely stretch of beach, the camera followed the final movements of Captain Gross, the group's leader. Fatally injured, his arm crept toward the picture of his wife and children that he always carried in his cap. As his hand fell limp short of its goal, the ocean washed up to claim both his body and the photograph of his family. The visual message of the episode spoke to the unity of the American family. What threatened one member, threatened all. Best-selling combat pictures of the war years underscored this American perception. According to these popular war movies, each family member had a significant function, whether husband, wife, mother, or child. And, the films intimated, survival of the nation depended upon them all.

For the military heroines who sent their men abroad, this often meant the arduous task of waiting patiently for news and, meanwhile, surviving on their own. Combat films of the war years suggested that women could handle these circumstances ably, and credit was given them for a swell performance of their duty.

Conclusion

Questions about Women's Culture and Social Change

Writing in 1942, sociologist Ernest W. Burgess suggested that the biggest change to be anticipated in American social patterns as a result of World War II was "a further rise in the status of women." Noting that World War I had given women "the outward symbols of equality with men"—including both the political right to suffrage and "a social freedom" which permitted short skirts, bobbed hair, drinking, and smoking—Burgess predicted that "the present war and the following reconstruction period" would offer American women "more of the substance of equality than did the last conflict." The University of Chicago professor based his supposition primarily on "the big increase in the number of working women." Drawing a direct equation, Burgess concluded that women's new earning power in the marketplace would hoist them into a position of "enhanced social status"—one that would be apparent in changed relationships within the home as well as in the public and private economic sectors of the nation.[1]

In his carefully researched, sometimes brilliant study of women's changing roles from 1920 to 1970, William Chafe found Burgess's prediction to be accurate. World War II was a "watershed event" for American women, Chafe wrote, for the war disrupted "traditional patterns of life" in significant and lasting ways. Before World War II, it had been almost unheard of for a middle-class wife or mother to work outside the home. The war changed this social pattern, eventually making work in the marketplace "the rule rather than the exception" for middle-class married women as well as lower-class wives and single females.[2]

According to Chafe, women's employment outside the home "operated as an effective engine of change in the lives of women," both during the war and into the reconstruction period. While economic and social equality remained a distant goal in the late 1940s, women's status had been permanently altered by the patriotic efforts of women during World War II. Females' experiences as workers in factories, businesses, and the professions had given them new confidence in the role of a bread-winner, leading to "a series of 'unanticipated' consequences in relations between the sexes." The most significant by-product of women's increased economic activity, Chafe suggested, was the redistribution of responsibilities within the home. Since most married women workers in the marketplace found "it difficult to carry a full-time job outside the home and still shoulder the burden of household management," justice required the husband to assume "at least some of the responsibilities previously borne by the wife." The husband-father's acceptance of the duties of "women's work" seldom happened quickly, Chafe maintained, but what began as a "favor" became, over time, a "routine"—then an "obligation."[3]

In short, the massive influx of women into the marketplace during World War II had accelerated, dramatically, the twentieth-century movement toward equality for American women—both in the home and in society. Women's proficiency in war jobs challenged extant work stereotypes, encouraging a reevaluation of men's and women's roles in private institutions such as the home and family as well as the more public areas of industry, business, and government.

Chafe attributed his theory of social change to historian Carl Degler. Paraphrasing Degler, Chafe wrote that social change (in the United States) is more likely to occur as a practical response to specific events than as the implementation of a well developed ideology. In other words, according to these historians and others, American women's status was more likely to improve as a result of a condition such as a wartime labor scarcity in the marketplace than as a reaction to a public dialogue generated by organizing women's groups who demanded justice for their sex and offered a blueprint for change. Their concept suggested that the experience of working next to a woman (or a minority person) on an assembly line or in an office altered Americans' behaviors toward those persons more readily than the speeches or writings of groups such as feminists or civil rights advocates, whose efforts were mainly directed at changing, through education or new government policy, the discriminatory attitudes ingrained in the public mind. Essentially a practical people, Americans responded to economic pressure and patriotic necessities rather than well developed ideologies.[4]

Of course, as Chafe pointed out, the interplay of attitude and behavior is very complicated. While World War II changed the realities of many American women's lives—legitimizing work outside the home for middle-class married women, a trend which "quickened rather than slowed during the post-war years," according to Chafe—traditional ideas about woman's place in American society remained fairly static. The female

who worked in the marketplace either from necessity or desire for ful-
fillment would not become a popular heroine in the nation's folklore until
the 1970s, after the women's movement had prompted a public reevaluation of women's position in society. In fact, the heroines whom the
public found acceptable in the years of the late forties and the decades
of the fifties and sixties were primarily domestic women who were contented with the occupation of housewives. Thus, in the eyes of some
observers, the war had a very different impact from the one suggested by
Chafe. Neither American women nor men had found their experiences
during the war liberating. At the war's end, men were eager to return to
their homes, families, and civilian jobs—and women were equally anxious
to resume their traditional roles. The popularity of the housewife-mother
figure in films, television programs, magazine short stories, and novels of
the post-war decades suggested that Americans of both sexes were willing
to pay tribute to this role.[5]

Since the process of social change would appear to include a new sense
of options on the part of second-class citizens as well as a new awareness
of their situation in the consciousness of people in the larger society,
World War II seems, in retrospect, less than the watershed event predicted by Burgess and described by Chafe. Despite the numerical increase
of women in the marketplace (encouraged by government agencies and
media slogans) women's definitions of themselves—and the public's perception of their primary responsibilities—changed hardly at all during the
war and the reconstruction period. Dramatic changes in Americans' attitudes toward women would wait another 20 years—until the Civil Rights
Movement of the 1960s provoked women to consider their position and
articulate their grievances.[6]

In the interim, American women and men expressed little discontent
with the social roles assigned them. Although Betty Friedan described
this period as one in which women tried to define "The Problem That
Has No Name," and William Chafe saw it as a time in which anti-feminist
ideas provided the backdrop for women's drive for equality in the late
1960s, I do not think that Americans' persistent affection for women's
culture is best described in these terms.[7]

Popular war movies produced in the years 1941–1945 revealed the
high esteem Americans attached to the domains of women when the institutions and values of the nation were threatened by an external enemy.
The evidence in best-selling feature films of the war years suggests that
America defined freedom for women as the right to vote and pursue a
career, but also as the opportunity to choose a husband and bear children

in a protected environment. For married women opportunity meant *not* working in the marketplace. Since the family was credited with being the most important institution in a democratic society, "the sacred spring from which the strength, the character and the virtue of our people find daily replenishment" (in President Roosevelt's words), women's caretaking functions were seen to demand their full attention, offering a pleasurable and important role to the wife and mother as well as a benefit to the husband-father and an investment to society. This definition of woman's place persisted in the public mind well into the 1970s, and advocates of this viewpoint are still vociferous in groups such as Fascinating Womanhood or The Total Woman.[8]

Motion picture top-grossing war movies of the World War II period tell us something about the components of women's culture which both women and men seemed to respect in that era. Most important, perhaps, was the female's perceived ability to be in charge of human relationships. Mothers such as Anne Hilton or Mother York were shown to understand their children in special ways, knowing just when to tolerate crushes or wild behavior while also being aware of the time for firmness. Similarly, wives or fiancees were depicted as the most important judges of their men's behavior—neither Tama nor Anna would accept a fascist as a lover, while Mrs. Miniver's praise of Clem or Gracie's loyalty to Alvin York revealed the propriety of their actions in war.

Women were also shown to speak a special language of compassion. They tactfully soothed hurt feelings, ably defended their men or children without rancor, supported the war effort as a necessary evil since they were devoted basically to peace, had comforting words to offer when tragedy or death occurred, and seldom expressed anger either verbally or in their demeanors.

Despite this type of classic fortitude, women characters in the popular war movies of the 1940s were not depicted as passive or helpless persons. While their major interests were described as romance, marriage, home, and family, these institutions were shown to be vital ones in the American structure and women were characterized as the persons in control of them. The patriarchal model often ascribed to American society was not evident in these films. Although men were the persons who mostly experienced combat or earned money in the marketplace, women were responsible for the family budgets and the maintenance of the home. While these roles have been described as limiting ones for women in our own time—with justice—the best-selling war pictures of World War II suggest that the American public had a different view in the 1940s.

The popular heroine of the war years—the woman who dominated in the folklore of the nation—was not "Rosie the Riveter," the working wife. Rather she was the woman, like Mrs. Miniver or Anne Hilton or Anna Muller, who defended her traditional domains and culture. Entering the war economy was, according to film evidence, only one phase of the patriotic effort expected of a good woman citizen. In this sense the war might be viewed as a conservative influence where women were concerned. Faced with a fascist enemy who wished to press women back to a medieval status, Americans placed great emphasis upon the liberated position of women in their own society.

The dominance of the image of the housewife-mother heroine in the post-war decades lends substance to this idea. In wartime propaganda, the nation's commitment to the war effort was defined partially in terms of the importance of women's position in the home and family. Thus Americans retained a strong loyalty to women's traditional roles after the war, even though marketplace statistics revealed that most women would hold a job outside the home at some point in their lives.[9]

Popular war movies of the years 1941–1945 disclosed an ambivalence toward women's roles and status that would continue to permeate American society through the post-war era. According to these films, women could perform the usual work of men efficiently and competently, but they chose to do so only in a national emergency, for their deeper commitment was to their husbands, families, and homes. Although surveys conducted at the end of the war indicated that women in the labor force found sufficient pleasure and meaning in their jobs to want to keep them, the working woman did not prevail as the popular image after the war.[10]

As the top-grossing films produced during World War II indicated, the war had actually bolstered Americans' belief in the importance of women's traditional domains. Until the women's movement of the 1970s forced a reconsideration of the gap between women's lives and popular images, the housewife-mother heroine remained the dominant image in American popular culture.

It is my contention that changing popular attitudes is a very important part of the process of social change. While women's experiences in the marketplace during World War II and the post-war years may have altered the day-to-day lifestyles of many Americans, without a public dialogue that addressed these issues and presented new directions, Americans mostly floundered, questioning their own behavior privately and clinging, rather tenaciously, to the traditional roles and patterns that had been lauded as acceptable, patriotic ones during a crisis period in the nation's history.

In the final analysis, women's culture does represent a work load which cannot be dismissed lightly. Since Americans continue to show no desire to abandon the institutions traditionally placed in women's care, the new feminine images on television reflect the public's attempt to find alternate models, ones which offer solutions to the troubling problems of combining men's and women's work on an equal and human basis.

Notes

Preface

1. Gail Rock chastises television for its limited attention to women in "Same Time, Same Station, Same Sexism," *Ms. Magazine* (December, 1973), p. 24. Beth Gutcheon suggests a different viewpoint in "TV: There's Nothing Wishy-Washy About Soaps," *Ms. Magazine* (August, 1974), p. 42.

2. Columbia Pictures producer Robert Sweeney (SFR Productions) spoke at length on the importance of ratings at a session of the West Coast Association of Women Historians (May 6, 1978). When asked to assess the impact of ratings on local television programming, a spokesman for Group W Westinghouse Broadcasting Company of Santa Barbara, Calif., said simply, "I live or die by them." (Interview, May 18, 1978).

3. Betty Friedan, *The Feminine Mystique* (New York, 1963). Quotations are taken from the Dell Edition (1975), pp. 32–38. Also see Beatrice K. Hofstadter's "Popular Culture and the Romantic Heroine," *The American Scholar*, Vol. 30, No. 1 (Winter, 1960–61), p. 98.

4. Betty Friedan, "Betty Friedan Reviews the Changing Image of Women," Santa Barbara *News-Press* (April 23, 1978), p. C-17.

5. Ibid.

6. Afternoon Session II, West Coast Association of Women Historians (May 6, 1978).

7. Andrew Bergman, *We're in the Money: Depression America and Its Films* (New York, 1971), p. xii. "The Social and Economic Status of the Black Population in the United States," Current Population Reports, Special Studies Series P-23, No. 54 (July, 1975), p. 139, Bureau of the Census, United States Department of Commerce.

8. For an especially provocative interpretation of the censorship issue, see Robert Sklar, *Movie-Made America: A Social History of American Movies* (New York, 1975).

9. John Blassingame spoke of the importance of utilizing fresh sources in tracing the history of black Americans in *The Slave Community: Plantation Life in the Antebellum South* (New York, 1972). For a good review of possible new sources for studying the past of American women, see Joanna Schneider Zangrando, "Women's Studies in the

United States: Approaching Reality," *American Studies International*, Vol. XIV, No. 1 (Autumn, 1975), p. 15.

10. In his introduction, Bergman notes the trends inspired by best-selling films in *We're in the Money*. The pioneer of scholarly work based on film evidence, Siegfried Kracauer, wrote, "To be sure, American audiences receive what Hollywood wants them to want; but in the long run public desires determine the nature of Hollywood films." *From Caligari to Hitler: A Psychological History of the German Film* (Princeton, 1947), p. 6.

11. For an excellent review of Rosen's and Haskell's books, read Stephen Farber's "The Vanishing Heroine," *The Hudson Review*, Vol. XXVII, No. 4 (Winter, 1974–75), p. 570.

12. Gerda Lerner, "New Approaches to the Study of Women in American History," *Journal of Social History*, Vol. III (1969), p. 53.

13. Eugene C. McCreary, "Film and History: Some Thoughts on Their Interrelationship," *Societas*, Vol. 1, No. 1 (Winter, 1971), p. 51.

14. Michael T. Isenberg, "A Relationship of Constrained Anxiety: Historians and Film," *The History Teacher*, Vol. VI, No. 4 (August, 1973), p. 553.

15. The quotation appears in William H. Chafe's *Women and Equality: Changing Patterns in American Culture* (Oxford, 1977), p. 11. For a look at the impact of the First Women's Movement on women's images, see Linda Harris Mehr, "Down Off The Pedestal: Some Modern Heroines in Popular Culture, 1890–1917" (Ph.D. diss., University of California, Los Angeles, 1973).

16. The Bureau of Motion Pictures (Domestic Branch) was not fully operative until the summer of 1942, and it was phased out the following year. Despite its short tenure in the Office of War Information, its records were very helpful to me in writing chapters 3 and 5.

17. Leo A. Handel, *Hollywood Looks at Its Audience: A Report of Film Audience Research* (Urbana, 1950), p. 31.

18. Barbara Deming, an analyst in the Library of Congress' Film Preservation Project in the 1940s, used the analyses of individual films' formats with convincing success in her *Running Away from Myself: A Dream Portrait of America Drawn from the Films of the Forties* (New York, 1969). This approach is also the one favored by scholars in film studies.

Introduction

1. The slogan was the insignia for a *Womanpower* pamphlet prepared by the war Advertising Council, Inc., in cooperation with the Office of War Information, War Manpower Commission Army-Navy Joint Personnel Board, February 15, 1944, Entry 90, Box 587, Records of the Office of War Information, Record Group 208, Washington National Records Center, Suitland, Md. (hereafter, RG, WNRC). For discussions of the war's impact on American women, see William H. Chafe, *The American Woman* (New York, 1972), pp. 135–195, Geoffrey Perrett, *Days of Sadness, Years of Triumph* (Baltimore,

1974), pp. 343–347, Richard Lingeman, *Don't You Know There's a War On?* (New York, 1970), pp. 148–159, and Peter G. Filene, *Him/Her/Self, Sex Roles in Modern America* (New York, 1976), pp. 168–172.

2. Eleanor Roosevelt's perspective is explained in a draft for an article for the *Metal Trades Council Review and Directory*, October 13, 1942, Eleanor Roosevelt Papers, File 3046, Franklin D. Roosevelt Library, Hyde Park, New York.

3. Wartime propaganda posters are reproduced in *This Fabulous Century, 1940–1950* (New York: Time-Life Books, 1969), pp. 142–193; Virginia Snow Wilkinson's article appears in *Harper's Magazine* (September, 1943), pp. 335–337.

4. Richard Lingeman explores radio's contributions to the war effort, and offers these quotations in *Don't You Know There's a War On?*, pp. 223–233. Radio CIO's broadcast, "The Bullet That's Going to Kill Hitler," was a typical dramatization designed to boost the egos of white collar workers, Win the War Script No. 4, June 12, 1942, Entry 264, File A, RG 208, WNRC.

5. For coverage of women in the armed forces, consult portions of the following Paramount Newsreels: May 19, 1942; July 24, 1942; August 18, 1942; September 1, 1942; "Meet the WAFs," September 25, 1942; October 13, 1942; "Rough Riders," November 10, 1942, RG 200, Motion Picture Division, National Archives. United News also featured the WACs (UN 63, 1943) and described child nurseries (UN 3, 1942), RG 208, Motion Picture Division, National Archives. For women in industry, see Paramount Newsreels of April 7, 1942; July 7, 1942; July 24, 1942; November 24, 1942; December 4, 1942.

6. See Lewis Jacobs' article, "World War II and the American Film," *Cinema Journal*, Vol. VII (Winter, 1967–68), reprinted in Arthur F. McClure, ed. *The Movies: An American Idiom* (New Jersey, 1971), pp. 153–177. Marjorie Rosen's *Popcorn Venus* (New York, 1973), section 4, and Molly Haskell's *From Reverence to Rape* (New York, 1973), chapter 5 are also valuable.

7. Chafe, *American Woman*, chapter 6.

8. Report by Eugene Katz, Special Services Division, to Cornelius Du Bois, executive assistant, "Preliminary Information on Women and the War Effort," July 14, 1942, Box 1842, Records of the Bureau of Intelligence, Records of the Office of Government Reports, RG 44, WNRC. Glenn L. Martin is quoted in LaVerne Bradley's "Women at Work," *The National Geographic Magazine*, Vol. LXXXVI, No. 2 (August, 1944), pp. 193–220. Eleanor Roosevelt's view appears in a draft for *Click Magazine*, "Women in the Post War," (August, 1944), ER Papers, File 3050, FDR Library.

9. Peter Filene suggests that "although the war drastically changed the activities of women, attitudes proved to be less elastic—and sex roles are determined by what people believe and expect as much as by what they do." *Him/Her/Self*, p. 169.

10. War Advertising Council *Womanpower* pamphlet, page two, (February 15, 1944), Entry 90, Box 587, RG 208, WNRC.

11. John M. Blum explores the efforts to make heroes from "the man in the street" in *V Was For Victory* (New York, 1976), Sections 1 and 2. The lack of government support for women workers is described in William H. Chafe's *The American Woman* (New York, 1972), chapters 7 and 8.

12. United News (UN 63, 1943), RG 208, Motion Picture Division, National Archives; Paramount News (September 1, 1942), RG 200 in the same locale.

13. According to John Blum, the pie's flavor was blueberry. See Blum's *V Was For Victory* (New York, 1976), p. 66. For attitudes of soldiers and others, read pages 94-95 in the same source, and Marjorie Rosen, *Popcorn Venus* (New York, 1973), Section 4.

14. F. Scott Fitzgerald, *The Last Tycoon* (New York, 1976), p. 137, originally published in 1941. The description of *Sergeant York* appeared in the cinema review section in *Time* (August 4, 1941), pp. 70–71.

Chapter One

1. For comparative theater grosses, see *Boxoffice Barometer*, Vol. 40, No. 14, Section 2 (February 21, 1942), pp. 41–49. *Sergeant York*'s and Gary Cooper's entwined fame was referred to by marines in *Guadalcanal Diary* (1943); a Southern sharpshooter, Tex, was asked to explain which man—Sergeant York or Gary Cooper—he was "playing" when rifle practicing in the jungles of Guadalcanal. Lowell Mellett's comments are recorded in a memorandum to Stephen T. Early, July 23, 1941, Lowell Mellett Papers, Box 6, Franklin D. Roosevelt Library, Hyde Park, N.Y.

2. Lewis Jacobs, "World War II and the American Film," *Cinema Journal*, Vol. VII (Winter, 1967–68).

3. Contemporary reviewers praised the film's authenticity. "I don't think the life in the backwoods of the South has ever been better described on the screen," John Mosher wrote in *New Yorker*. ". . . [The film is] a documented, careful account of Alvin York's early days which made him so fit a soldier." *New Yorker* (July 5, 1941), p. 43. *Newsweek* (July 4, 1941), pp. 61–62 and *Time* (August 4, 1941), pp. 70–71 shared Mosher's opinion.

4. John Mosher described Mother York as "an Erskine Caldwell character with dignity," and further suggested that the movie's depiction of courtship provided novelty from the usual "perfunctory sentimental theme" in films. *New Yorker* (July 5, 1941), p. 43.

5. All quotations in this synopsis (as well as others that follow) were transcribed from the soundtracks of the movies themselves. This kind of close attention to film detail was possible because of the excellent research facilities in the Library of Congress as well as the University of California, Los Angeles. The essential machine in this process, the Steenbeck projector, allows the viewer control of a film. Since I could stop the movie in progress—or go forward or backward at my own pace—I was able to record the content of films in detail, thus providing myself with written evidence. This kind of thorough acquaintance with each popular movie in my sample seemed necessary to a fair evaluation of the images of women in each. The synopses are included to offer the reader the same degree of familiarity, although the film has been filtered, of course, through my impressions.

6. As the major box-office draw of the year, *Sergeant York* received extensive critical attention. See *Catholic World* (October, 1941), p. 86; *Commonweal* (July 18, 1941), p. 306; *Life* (July 14, 1941), pp. 63–65; *New Republic* (September 29, 1941), pp. 404–405; *New Yorker* (July 5, 1941), p. 43; *Newsweek* (July 14, 1941), pp. 61–62; *Scholastic* (September 15, 1941), p. 28; *Time* (August 4, 1941), p. 70.

7. Lewis Jacobs points to *Sergeant York*'s war preparedness qualities in "World War II and the American Film," *Cinema Journal* (Winter, 1967–68). For comments on war's impact on sexual roles, read Filene's *Him/Her/Self*, chapters 4 and 6.

8. Since Hollywood producers conscientiously dealt in folklore rather than reality, this type of omission might be anticipated in an adventure, comedy, or usual dramatic film of the pre-World War II years. *Sergeant York*, however, was undertaken as a "patriotic duty" (*Newsweek*, July 14, 1941), p. 62, and one might expect more of a documentary of women's lives, as well as men's.

9. The literature recounting the debate on "woman's place" during the first 20 years of this century is extensive. One might begin with Eleanor Flexner, *Century of Struggle: The Women's Rights Movement in the United States* (New York, 1972)—originally published in 1959—for historical perspective, and then consult William O'Neill, *Everyone Was Brave* (Chicago, 1971), and June Sochen, editor, *The New Feminism in Twentieth Century America* (Lexington, 1971) for interpretations, primary sources, and bibliography. The quotation from Anne Martin is found in a letter to Mrs. Tiny G. Kemble (October 24, 1916), Anne Martin Collection, Bancroft Library, University of California, Berkeley.

10. Flexner, *Century of Struggle*, p. 323.

11. Ibid., especially chapters 20 and 21. Also on women's suffrage, one should not miss Aileen S. Kraditor's *The Ideas of the Woman Suffrage Movement* (Garden City, 1971).

12. Women's varied activities in the Progressive Reform Era are synthesized in Lois Banner's *Women in Modern America: A Brief History* (New York, 1974), section 3. The pre-World War I shift in women's behavior is postulated in James R. McGovern's article "The American Woman's Pre-World War I Freedom in Manner and Morals," *Journal of American History* (September, 1968).

13. For an account of opposition to the 19th Amendment, see Kraditor, *The Ideas of the Woman Suffrage Movement* and Flexner, *Century of Struggle*, especially chapter 22. Filene's *Him/Her/Self* is instructive in the perceived domains of men and women in this period.

14. Charlotte Perkins Gilman, *Women and Economics* (Boston, 1898), p. 222. During her lifetime Gilman's books were welcomed by both publishers and readers, and she has also received recent attention from scholars. See particularly Carl N. Degler's "Charlotte Perkins Gilman on the Theory and Practice of Feminism," *American Quarterly* (Spring, 1956), pp. 21–39.

15. Women's activities during World War I receive brief attention in Filene's *Him/Her/Self*, Flexner's *Century of Struggle*, and Banner's *Women in Modern America*. Protesting

suffragists are more thoroughly described in Inez Haynes Irwin's *Up Hill with Banners Flying* (Penobscot, Maine, 1964)—originally published in 1921—and in Janice Law Trecker's article, "The Suffrage Prisoners," *American Scholar* (Summer, 1972), pp. 409–429.

16. Tamera K. Hareven discusses the importance of the family unit and delineates sexual roles in an agrarian society in "The History of the Family as an Interdisciplinary Field," *Journal of Interdisciplinary History* (Fall, 1971).

17. Elizabeth Cady Stanton, *Eighty Years and More* (New York, 1898), pp. 147–148.

18. In the film, Mother York was the only person who showed an awareness of generations or a continuum of family life. The effect of her knowledge seemed basically conservative—since Alvin's father had failed in his attempt to obtain bottomland, so would her son. Yet the burden of history had not forced Mother York into a final verdict; despite her sense of past failures, she could still encourage her son. As the symbol of wisdom in the movie, Mother York believed in the American Dream of upward mobility.

19. Cinema review, *Time* (August 4, 1941), p. 71.

20. Other best-sellers of 1941 reflected the contrasting perceptions of women in the public mind. Images of the "new woman" were glimpsed in *Philadelphia Story*, *A Yank in the RAF*, and even *Life Begins for Andy Hardy*, while women stood by their men in classic fashion in *How Green Was My Valley* and *Honky Tonk*. See footnote No. 32 for a complete listing of the most popular films of 1941.

21. The description of *Confessions of a Nazi Spy* is found in Jacobs, "World War II and the American Film." For Wheeler's statement and an account of the political attention pre-World War II films elicited, see Lingeman, *Don't You Know There's a War On?*, Chapter VI.

22. Jacobs, "World War II and the American Film," and Joel Greenberg and Charles Higham, *Hollywood in the Forties* (London, 1968), chapter 6.

23. In the movie, John Doe, alias Long John Willoughby, became sufficiently newsworthy to appear on *Time*'s cover. On the magazine's 18th anniversary, the editors recognized both Gary Cooper and Capra's film by featuring Cooper as John Doe in a cover story (March 3, 1941), pp. 78–82. The reference to Ann Mitchell (Barbara Stanwyck) is found in John Mosher's "Meet the Messiah," a film review in *New Yorker* (March 22, 1941), p. 64.

24. Earlier Capra films devoted to "the little man" included *Mr. Deeds Goes to Town* (1936), *You Can't Take It with You* (1938), and *Mr. Smith Goes to Washington* (1939). Capra's (and screenwriter, Robert Riskin's) "love of the common man . . . passeth all understanding," John Mosher observed in *New Yorker* (March 22, 1941), p. 64. Their formula produced sure money at the box-office, however, suggesting that Capra and Riskin were masters at portraying Americans as they wished to think of themselves.

25. Capra shot five different endings to *Meet John Doe*. See chapter 16 in his autobiography, *The Name Above the Title* (New York, 1971).

26. *Newsweek*'s critic praised the uplifting ending of *Meet John Doe*, suggesting that the movie's "faith in democracy and the garden variety of American" was "as timely as news from the English Channel . . ." (March 24, 1941), p. 69.

27. Americans who lived it reminisce about the depression in Studs Terkel's oral history, *Hard Times* (New York, 1970). For information on income distribution at the end of the thirties, read Douglas C. North, *Growth and Welfare in the American Past: A New Economic History* (New Jersey, 1966).

28. *Time* noted that "the biggest Capra-Riskin picture to date" was built "around one of the simplest and oldest of themes: Love Thy Neighbor," (March 3, 1941), p. 78. This sermon was delivered by a master technician, suggested Joel Greenberg and Charles Higham. The film offered "its naive utopian message . . . with such dazzling cinematic panache that, watching it, even the most cynical realist must succumb to its enchantment." *Hollywood in the Forties*, p. 72.

29. Bergman discusses newspaper people's (and other city shysters') corruption of the American success story in *We're in the Money*, chapter 2.

30. This was an unusual combination of male/female protagonists in Hollywood films. Even the dynamic Rosalind Russell had a more even match (Cary Grant) in the most famous of women reporter films, *His Girl Friday* (1940). The "breezy sob sister" was, however, a favorite movie character in the thirties and early forties, suggesting that women had made a mark, by this time, in the journalistic world. See Haskell, *From Reverence to Rape*, "The Thirties."

31. It is important to note that—although the film offered no explicit information—critics in 1941 interpreted Ann Mitchell's actions as a "surrender of love." Evidently, at that time, a career and marriage did not mix for women, even in the minds of the intelligentsia. See especially Mosher's review, *New Yorker* (March 22, 1941), p. 64.

32. Five films were cross-listed as top box-office draws in the available sources on movie revenues: *Sergeant York*, *Philadelphia Story*, *Honky Tonk*, *The Great Dictator*, *Hold That Ghost*. Nine others received mention in two sources: *Caught in the Draft*, *Charley's Aunt*, *Yank in the RAF*, *Road to Zanzibar*, *Life Begins for Andy Hardy*, *Meet John Doe*, *How Green Was My Valley*, *Louisiana Purchase*, and *Nothing but the Truth*. Other than *Sergeant York* and *Meet John Doe*, the only films to treat fascism were *The Great Dictator* (set in a mythical country) and *Yank in the RAF*. *Caught in the Draft* starred Bob Hope as an eager draft evader who eventually accepted his patriotic duty in order to "win" Dorothy Lamour, who would have "none of a slacker and coward." *Newsweek* (July 7, 1941), p. 50. For listings of "best sellers," see *Boxoffice Barometer*, Vol. 40, No. 14, Section 2, (February 21, 1942), pp. 41–49, Paul Michael, ed. *The American Movies Reference Book, The Sound Era* (Englewood Cliffs, New Jersey, 1969), p. 618 and Terry Ramsaye, ed. *The International Motion Picture Almanac* (New York, 1942), pp. 1120–1121.

33. John Mosher, Cinema review, *New Yorker* (July 5, 1941), p. 43.

34. The quotation—and an extended discussion of the anti-suffragists' philosophy—appears in Kraditor's *The Ideas of the Woman Suffrage Movement*, chapter 2.

35. Movies had probed these areas more freely in the twenties and early thirties. Ironically, women's groups provided much of the clout behind the enforcement of censorship codes in the 1930s. See Ruth A. Inglis, *Freedom of the Movies* (Chicago, 1947).

36. Cinema review, *Time* (June 29, 1942), p. 72. For comments on "women's films," see Rosen, *Popcorn Venus*, chapter 12.

Chapter Two

1. Geoffrey Perrett observes that Americans "expected the war to last two or three years." He also notes that after Pearl Harbor, "something of a family feeling prevailed" in the United States. Americans "were openly thankful for the newfound feelings of national unity and purpose." *Days of Sadness, Years of Triumph: The American People 1939-1945* (Baltimore, 1974), p. 205.

2. Lowell Mellett also expressed the government's confidence in the film community's ability to not "goose-step the American soul." "The Government and Motion Pictures," March 4, 1943, Entry 264, Box 1433, Records of the Office of War Information, RG 208, WNRC. On a more personal level, Mrs. Wenona Baker, a young woman in her twenties during World War II, mentioned the importance of movies in making the war real to her and other persons in her rural Colorado community. Interview, February, 1975, Garden City, Kansas.

3. John Mosher, "Over There," Cinema Review, *New Yorker* (June 6, 1942), p. 60. Audience identification with film characters and male and female stars is explored in Leo A. Handel's *Hollywood Looks at Its Audience: A Report of Film Audience Research* (Urbana, 1950).

4. Manny Farber, "War Horses," Cinema Review, *New Republic* (June 15, 1942), p. 830.

5. Cinema Review, *Time* (June 29, 1942), p. 72.

6. "Mrs. Miniver's War," Cinema Review, *Newsweek* (June 15, 1942), p. 63.

7. John Mosher, p. 60.

8. For a description of public attitudes in the months before war, see Robert Groves and Alan Hodge, *The Long Week-End: A Social History of Great Britain, 1918-1939* (New York, 1963)—first published in 1941—chapter 26.

9. In *Time* magazine's critic's words: "Tomorrow will always balance the books," (June 29, 1942), p. 72.

10. Bureaucrats in the Bureau of Motion Pictures, Office of War Information praised the leveling of the aristocracy in *Mrs. Miniver*, noting that the picture was promoting the United Nation's war objectives when "the dowager Lady Beldon is made to realize that her stake in the outcome of the war is just as great as that of the 'common people' whom she has always looked down upon." Bureau of Motion Pictures' *Evaluation of Motion Pictures*, p. 3, Entry 264, Box 1438, Records of the OWI, RG 208, WNRC.

11. Analyst Dorothy Jones, "Character Analysis—Mr. Ballard," *Feature and Serial Analysis* (May 29, 1942), *Mrs. Miniver File*, Motion Picture Feature Film Archive, Library of Congress.

12. Vin is described in this manner in the "Plot" segment of the *Feature and Serial Analysis*.

13. Analyst Jones wrote, "It (*Mrs. Miniver*) admits the existence of class distinctions before the war, but indicates that such barriers have been broken down to form the people into a cooperating and mutually sympathetic unit."

14. The broadcast occurred at 11:15 on Sunday morning, September 3, 1939. Americans who had recently received shattering news on the Sunday of December 7, 1941, could identify easily with the British. See Robert Graves and Alan Hodge, *The Long Week-End*, p. 454 for an account of Prime Minister Neville Chamberlain's speech to the English nation.

15. The period of the "phoney war" is described in A. J. P. Taylor's *English History 1914–1945* (New York, 1965), pp. 453–475.

16. Manny Farber called this scene "a director's dream," in his review in *New Republic* (June 15, 1942), p. 831, and *Time*'s critic was equally complimentary (June 29, 1942), p. 72.

17. Critic Farber, who described *Mrs. Miniver* as a "not very good" picture which "has all the things that win Academy awards," insisted that "the letdown is terrific as we return home to Mrs. Miniver." Other reviewers were more generous, evidently finding the home front as worthy of interest as the action in the Channel.

18. Analyst Dorothy Jones, "Character Analysis—German Flier," *Feature and Serial Analysis* (May 29, 1942), *Mrs. Miniver File*, Motion Picture Feature Film Archive, Library of Congress.

19. Cinema Review, *Time* (June 19, 1942), p. 72.

20. Geoffrey Perrett describes Americans' low morale during the first year of war in *Days of Sadness, Years of Triumph*, chapter 16.

21. Four films were listed as top box-office hits of 1942 in the available sources: C. B. DeMille's *Reap the Wild Wind* (Paramount); *Eagle Squadron* (Wanger, Universal); *Yankee Doodle Dandy* (Warners); *Mrs. Miniver* (MGM). *Box-Office Barometer*, Vol. 42, No. 16. Section 2 (February 27, 1943), pp. 45–49. Terry Ramsaye, ed., *International Motion Picture Almanac*, pp. 1120–1121; Paul Michael, ed., *The American Movies Reference Book, The Sound Era*, p. 618.

22. In addition to the war films mentioned in the text, movies listed as top box-office draws of 1942 in two sources included: *My Favorite Blond* (Paramount); *My Gal Sal* (20th Century-Fox); *In This Our Life* (WB); *Kings Row* (WB); *Woman of the Year* (MGM); *Holiday Inn* (Paramount); *Somewhere I'll Find You* (MGM); *Road to Morocco* (Paramount).

23. Richard Lingeman discusses the general American panic regarding saboteurs and invaders in *Don't You Know There's a War On?*, chapter 2.

24. Ibid;, p. 192. "Among the British intelligentsia . . ." Lingeman writes, "the picture was held to be a distortion of British middle-class life and British life in general." Of course British critics were right, for *Mrs. Miniver* was basically a film about American society. Even so, Lingeman reports, "London audiences were brought to tears by the movie, swallowing the film's sentimentality whole and accepting it as an American pat on the back for their sacrifices."

25. Betty Friedan discusses the emergence of the "Happy Housewife Heroine" of the 1940s in *The Feminine Mystique*, especially chapter 2. Novels of the time also contained heroines similar to Mrs. Miniver; see particularly, Judith Kelly's *Marriage Is a Private Affair* (New York, 1941), the Harper Prize winner of 1941.

26. Paul Rotha and Richard Griffin, editors, *The Film Till Now* (New York, 1951), pp. 438–439. Also see Andrew Bergman, *We're in the Money*, chapter 4, for a short analysis of women in films of the 1930s.

27. See chapter 1 of this work, pp. 00 and 00.

28. This message in the film seems especially significant since Americans were just beginning to enjoy the consumer role after years of depression hardship. Of course, the nation's economic recovery—and people's new jobs and high salaries—were linked to the building of a war machine, but citizens deprived of the pleasures of consuming for a decade were reluctant to confront this fact, as the flourishing black market in the country illustrated. See Lingeman, *Don't You Know There's a War On?*, chapter 7.

29. John Mosher, "Over There," p. 60.

30. Marjorie Rosen, *Popcorn Venus*, pp. 204–205.

31. "Women at War," Fact Sheet No. 15 (December 5, 1942), pp. 12 and oversheet, Hollywood Office, Bureau of Motion Pictures, Record of the Office of War Information, Entry 264, Box 1433F, RG 208, WNRC.

32. Ibid., p. 9.

33. Ibid., p. 3.

Chapter Three

1. For a listing of the top box-office hits of 1941, see footnote 32, chapter 1; for 1942, see footnotes 22 and 23, chapter 2. While the records for those years are clear, there is only minor overlapping of top-grossing movie titles of 1943 in the same sources. *Boxoffice Barometer* changed its format in 1944, publishing its yearly evaluation in November rather than February, and lumping together the movie grosses of 1943–44. In this process, the magazine appears to have ignored some major films listed in Paul Michael's edited work and *The International Motion Picture Almanac*. Since there is little agreement among the major sources, the list of top-grossing movies is much longer in 1943.

Statistics may have been more difficult to collect at this stage of the war—or the more extensive number of popular movies might simply reflect the "new high mark for business done at the nation's boxoffices," which *Boxoffice Barometer* happily reported, Vol. 46, No. 1 (November 11, 1944), p. 12.

2. In addition to the war films listed in the text, the best-sellers of 1943 included several others that hinted of the fascist threat or other aspects of World War II. These included *For Whom the Bell Tolls* (Paramount), an adaptation of Ernest Hemingway's novel, *Keeper of the Flame* (MGM), a Katherine Hepburn-Spencer Tracy vehicle which cast Hepburn as the murderess of her fascist husband, and two films that praised American allies—*The White Cliffs of Dover* (MGM) and *The North Star* (RKO). On the home front, United States gangsters were shown to be patriots under their hard veneer in *Lucky Jordan* (Paramount) and *Mr. Lucky* (RKO), while *Let's Face It* (Paramount) lampooned army life. *The More the Merrier* (Columbia) used the wartime housing shortages in Washington, D.C. as its comedy theme. The other popular films of 1943 made no direct references to the war: *Claudia* (20th Century-Fox); *Coney Island* (20th Century-Fox); *Dixie* (Paramount); *Heaven Can Wait* (20th Century-Fox); *Hers to Hold* (Universal); *Random Harvest* (MGM); *Girl Crazy* (MGM); *The Gang's All Here* (20th Century-Fox); *Madame Curie* (MGM); *Sweet Rosie O'Grady* (20th); *A Lady Takes a Chance* (RKO); *Hello, Frisco, Hello* (20th). Ibid.

3. *Hitler's Children* was adapted from Gregor Ziemer's best-selling non-fiction work, *Education For Death* (1941) while *Behind the Rising Sun* was based on correspondent James R. Young's book of the same name. Cinema Review, *Life* (February 1, 1943), p. 37; *Newsweek* (August 23, 1943), p. 86.

4. Cinema Review, *Newsweek* (August 23, 1943), p. 86.

5. Charles Higham and Joel Greenberg, *Hollywood in the Forties*, p. 89.

6. "Fact Sheet No. 15," (December 5, 1942), p. 14, Section IV, *War Information Manual*, Entry 264, Box 1433F, Records of the Office of War Information, RG 208, WNRC.

7. William Bayer, *The Great Movies* (New York, 1973), p. 137.

8. Bayer numbers *Casablanca* among the 60 great movies in cinema history, ibid. Also Charles Higham and Joel Greenberg praise *Casablanca* in *Hollywood in the Forties*, p. 19, suggesting that "Michael Curtiz . . . brought to life a nocturnal America of the imagination whose wholly American drive, energy and flair expressed themselves in the Forties' most characteristic single film, the unforgettable *Casablanca*."

9. Philip T. Hartung, "War Evaluation," *Feature and Serial Analysis* (January 4, 1943), *Casablanca File*, Motion Picture Feature Film Archive, Library of Congress.

10. Analysts in the OWI praised the character of Sam (portrayed by Dooley Wilson), pointing out that *Casablanca* contained scenes which showed "mutual respect between the negro and the white American." "Casablanca," *Weekly Summary and Analysis of Feature Motion Pictures*, Media Division, Bureau of Intelligence, OWI, Box 1845, Records of the Office of Government Reports, RG 44, WNRC.

11. Renault's depiction is seen as "possibly objectionable" because he "plays along with the Germans" and pursues pretty women in an unscrupulous manner. Ibid.

12. Rick is on the Nazi blacklist as a result of his activities in Ethiopia and Spain.

13. Immediately after this patriotic display, Captain Renault, under pressure from Major Strasser, closes Rick's cabaret. Thus viewers were informed of the fate of free speech in Nazi-dominated territories.

14. *Time*'s critic noted that the U.S. seizure of Morocco had "handed Warner Brothers some of the most dazzling promotion in years. . . ." (November 30, 1942).

15. Philip T. Hartung, "Character Analysis—Yvonne," *Feature and Serial Analysis* (January 4, 1943), *Casablanca File*, Motion Picture Feature Film Archive, Library of Congress.

16. The distinction is rather obvious in both the dialogue and in the gazing between couples. Laszlo expresses his love for Ilsa freely, while she responds to him with phrases such as "Be careful." With Rick, Ilsa is the one who speaks of loving.

17. "Feature Films and OWI Campaigns and Programs," (February, 1943), p. 5, Media Division, Bureau of Intelligence, OWI, Box 1845, Records of the Office of Government Reports, RG 44, WNRC.

18. "Feature Films and OWI Campaigns and Programs," (January, 1943), p. 9.

19. "Feature Films and OWI Campaigns and Programs," (January, 1943), p. 5.

20. Ibid.

21. "Hitler's Children," *Weekly Summary and Analysis of Feature Motion Pictures*, pp. 16–17, Media Division, Bureau of Intelligence, OWI, Box 1945, Records of the Office of Government Reports, RG 44, WNRC.

22. Marjorie Rosen, *Popcorn Venus*, p. 202. Also see *The Hollywood Reporter* (December 29, 1943), p. 3.

23. "Fact Sheet No. 15," (December 5, 1942), p. 3, Section IV, *War Information Manual*, Entry 264, Box 1433F. Records of the Office of War Information, RG 208, WNRC.

24. *New Yorker*'s reviewer, David Lardner, criticized the film's treatment of this major theme, suggesting that there was "more to the process (of Nazi indoctrination) than can be bludgeoned into us by means of a couple of good, ghoulish atrocity stories." "Swinging From the Floor," Cinema Review, *New Yorker* (March 6, 1943), p. 54. *Life*'s pictorial feature on *Hitler's Children* presented a different evaluation, claiming that "RKO has made a motion picture which is almost documentary in form." *Life* (February 1, 1943), p. 37.

25. Adolph Hitler was named chancellor of Germany on January 30, 1933. The film's depiction of the swift impact of Nazism on German life was actually quite realistic; see William L. Shirer, *The Rise and Fall of the Third Reich* (New York, 1960), chapter 7.

26. The teenagers' actions in this scene are easily read as an analogy of American-German foreign relations. The Americans fight only in self-defense while the Germans' main goal is to provoke a violent argument.

27. The character of Professor Nichols is based on the author, Gregor Ziemer, who was headmaster of the American Colony School in Berlin during the 1930s. *Life* magazine reported that "Ziemer with the permission of the Nazi Minister of Education studied at firsthand all phases of the Nazi educational machine." *Life* (February 1, 1943), p. 37.

28. Ibid., p. 37.

29. Ziemer recorded a different ending to this episode in his book, *Education For Death*, writing that "Even his (the boy's) Spartan spirit broke under the strain" of such treatment. Ibid., p. 39.

30. OWI analysts noted that German soldiers, while arrogant and fanatic, were "scarcely ever depicted as cruel or barbarous." In contrast, "The Japanese soldier is not as soldierly as the German and is often shown as cruel and ruthless . . . [since] he is not of our race, no peace is possible, he can only be killed." "The Enemy in the Movies," Special Intelligence Report No. 77 (November 25, 1942), p. 3, Media Division, BOI, OWI, Box 1845, RG 44, WNRC.

31. "Hitler's Children," *Weekly Summary and Analysis of Feature Motion Pictures*, pp. 16–17.

32. *The Hollywood Reporter*, (Tuesday, December 29, 1942), p. 3.

33. "Exhibit A," Appendage to letter from Nelson Poynter to Arch A. Mercey (April 29, 1943), Records of the OWI, Entry 264, Box 1437, RG 208, WNRC.

34. Letter from Nelson Poynter to Maurice Evans (May 8, 1943), Records of the OWI, Entry 264, Box 1437, RG 208, WNRC.

35. "Women in the War Effort," *Miscellaneous Feature Film Information File*, Records of the Correspondence between the Museum of Modern Art and the Library of Congress, Motion Picture Feature Film Archive, Library of Congress.

36. Insert to the *Government Information Manual*, OWI (April 29, 1943), pp. 14–15. Entry 264, Box 1433F, RG 208, WNRC.

37. "Fact Sheet No. 15," (December 5, 1942), pp. 3–9, Section IV, *War Information Manual*, Entry 264, Box 1433F, RG 208, WNRC.

38. The film insisted that the Nazi state went further than restricting women to the home. In *Hitler's Children*, women were basically breeders for the New Order, and they were denied the protection of their traditional spheres.

39. *The Hollywood Reporter* (Tuesday, December 29, 1942), p. 3.

40. "Hitler's Children," *Weekly Summary and Analysis of Feature Motion Pictures*, pp. 16–17.

41. Evidently, in 1943, laws prohibiting abortions were not perceived as state interference in childbearing decisions.

42. The claim that the film was based on "verified and authenticated facts" appears in writing at the beginning of the movie. The reviewer for *Time* thought the feature a propaganda piece, which was designed "to make Americans madder at the Japs than they are anyhow." Cinema Review, *Time* (August 9, 1943), p. 94. Other films mentioned by Poynter as giving "a serious interpretation of the enemy" rather than picturing him "as a villain or as a spy or saboteur" included RKO's *This Land Is Mine* and *Hitler's Children*; Warner's *Edge of Darkness*; 20th's *The Moon Is Down*; Columbia's *The Commando Strike at Dawn*; UA's *Hangmen Also Die* and MGM's *A Thousand Shall Fall*. Memorandum from Nelson Poynter to Lowell Mellett, "Trends in Hollywood Pictures" (June 1, 1943), p. 1. Entry 264, Box 1437, RG 208, WNRC.

43. Letter from Nelson Poynter to Arch Mercey (April 29, 1943), appended material, "Yardstick for War Pictures-" II—The Enemy. Entry 264, Box 1437, RG 208, WNRC.

44. Cinema Reviews, *Time* (August 9, 1943), p. 94; *Newsweek* (August 23, 1943), p. 87. For an evaluation of the image of Japanese soldiers in wartime movies, see "The Enemy in the Movies," Special Intelligence Report No. 77 (November 25, 1942), p. 3, Media Division, BOI, OWI, Box 1845, RG 44, WNRC.

45. Cinema Review, *New Yorker* (October 16, 1943), p. 44. Although John Toland's *The Rising Sun: The Decline and Fall of the Japanese Empire* is largely seen from the Japanese point of view, it is an immensely readable and thorough account of the years before and during World War II.

46. The Doolittle Raid of Task Force 16 was immortalized in a best selling war film of 1944, MGM's *Thirty Seconds Over Tokyo*.

47. John Toland suggests that the Japanese were not the only Orientals who resented the "white man's dominance." One of "America's greatest mistakes in World War II" was, he writes, the failing to recognize that millions of Asians saw "Japan's battle as their own, as a confrontation of race and color." *The Rising Sun*, p. xiv.

48. Of course the actual history of American attitudes toward the Japanese reveals a great amount of racial chauvinism. See Roger Daniels, *The Politics of Prejudice* (New York, 1970) and Audrie Girdner and Anne Loftis, *The Great Betrayal* (New York, 1969).

49. Cinema Reviews, *New Yorker* (October 16, 1943), p. 44; *Time* (August 9, 1943), p. 94.

50. Ken D. Jones and Arthur F. McClure, *Hollywood at War: The American Motion Picture and World War II* (New York, 1973), p. 15.

51. Leo A. Handel's audience research studies in the 1940s revealed that "70 percent of the people who go up to the box office to buy a ticket know what picture they are going to see" and that the majority of movie patrons interviewed mentioned word-of-mouth advertising as the most influential factor in their choice of films. *Hollywood Looks at Its Audience*, p. 151 and pp. 65–70.

52. There is reason to believe that BMP officials simply "gave up" on the issue of the Japanese-Americans, finding their situation too explosive to handle. In an article in the *Journal of American History*, Vol. LXIV, No. 1 (June, 1977) pp. 87–105, Clayton R. Koppes and Gregory D. Black describe an earlier, futile attempt by Nelson Poynter and the BMP staff to influence 20th Century-Fox's treatment of American citizens of Japanese ancestry in the movie, *Little Tokio, U.S.A.* (1942). Although the BMP began by vigorously protesting the depiction of Japanese-Americans as an "Invitation to the Witch Hunt," the sturdy resistance of the film's producer, Colonel Jason Joy, resulted in Poynter's capitulation. When *Little Tokio, U.S.A.* reached American audiences, footage of the actual evacuation of Los Angeles' Japanese was presented as a patriotic event, necessary "to save America." The BMP was less timid (or the American public more responsive) where other racial and ethnic groups were concerned. Various film analyses record a consistent interest in the images of black Americans, Italian Americans, and the Chinese.

53. "Main Street Calling," Radio Script, Box 1659, Records of the Office of Government Reports, RG 44, WNRC.

54. For a succinct discussion of the public dialogue on woman's "pacifistic nature," see Lois W. Banner, *Women in Modern America*, chapters 3 & 4. Dorothy Thompson's comments, originally published in 1941, are also instructive; read *Liberty* magazine (Summer, 1976), pp. 30–31.

55. Marie Louise Degen, *The History of the Woman's Peace Party* (Baltimore, 1939), p. 20.

Chapter Four

1. For a general discussion of the "women's pictures" of the war years that did not reach top box-office status, see Marjorie Rosen, *Popcorn Venus*, chapter 12. An analysis of the attributes of women based on secondary characters in war films is included in chapter 5 of this work.

2. Selznick's ambitions for the film were recorded in his lengthy memoranda. Read Rudy Behlmer, editor, *Memo from: David O. Selznick* (New York, 1972), pp. 381–391. Agee's comment appeared in his review of *Since You Went Away* in *Time* (July 17, 1944). Agee also critiqued the movie for *Nation* (July 29, 1944). Both reviews can be read in the collected work, *Agee on Film: Reviews and Comments by James Agee* (New York, 1969), pp. 106–108 and pp. 349–351.

3. Agee, *Agee on Film*, pp. 349–351.

4. Ibid., pp. 106–108.

5. Manny Farber wrote that Selznick was "finicky . . . about almost any object that would go into middle-class life," and "fiendishly finicky about mementoes," in a highly critical review of *Since You Went Away* in *New Republic* (July 17, 1944), p. 77. John Lardner described the Hilton residence as a "genteel home" in *New Yorker* (July 29, 1944), p. 44.

6. Movie review, "First GWTW, now SYWA," *Newsweek* (July 10, 1944), pp. 85–86.

7. "Government Information Manual," Bureau of Motion Pictures, Office of War Information (March 29, 1943), p. 15, Entry 264, Box 1433F, RG 208, WNRC. McDaniel's portrayal of Fidelia was certainly reminiscent of her "Mammy" in *Gone With the Wind*, Selznick's most famous picture.

8. For a description of wartime housing conditions, read Lingeman, *Don't You Know There's a War On?* chapter 3.

9. *Newsweek* (July 10, 1944), p. 86.

10. "Movie of the Week," *Life* (July 24, 1944), pp. 53–55.

11. Ibid.

12. Ibid.

13. Letter from Maurice Revnes to Nelson Poynter (May 5, 1943), Entry 264, Box 1437, RG 208, WNRC.

14. *Life* (July 24, 1944), p. 53.

Chapter Five

1. "Statement by the President," May 16, 1943, Official File 25 - JJ, FDR Library. Roosevelt's final statement was written from a draft submitted to Stephen P. Early (the president's secretary) by WAAC Director, Oveta Culp Hobby.

2. Lingeman, *Don't You Know There's a War On?*, pp. 154–55; Geoffrey Perrett, *Days of Sadness, Years of Triumph*, pp. 345–346; Letter from Harriet Elliot to Mary Dewson which Dewson passed on to her "boss," President Roosevelt, with the suggestion: "If the Navy gentlemen wish to give the women official status, why not? Gosh, it is mighty irksome to be an auxilliery [*sic*]." May 30, 1942, Official File 379-B, FDR Library.

3. Paramount Newsreels May 19, 1942; July 7, 1942; July 24, 1942; September 25, 1942; November 10, 1942; December 4, 1942; Draft of an article for *The Readers' Digest*, 1943, Eleanor Roosevelt Papers 3050, FDR Library.

4. Paramount Newsreels August 18, 1942; September 1, 1942; United News 208, 1943, Motion Picture Division, National Archives.

5. See particularly *Buck Privates* (Universal, 1941), *Private Buckaroo* (Universal, 1942), *Cry Havoc* (MGM, 1943), *A Guy Named Joe* (MGM-Loews, 1944), *Here Come the*

WAVES (Paramount, 1945). More than 100,000 American women were in military uniform during World War II.

6. The dialogue quotation from *Here Come the WAVES* was taken from the movie soundtrack, as are all subsequent quotations of movie characters in the chapter.

7. Draft of an article for *The Readers' Digest*, 1943, Eleanor Roosevelt Papers 3050, FDR Library.

8. Letter marked "personal and confidential," from Lowell Mellett to Nelson Poynter, December 30, 1942, Mellett Papers, Box 16, FDR Library.

9. Richard D. MacCann, *The People's Films: A Political History of U.S. Government Motion Pictures* (New York, 1973); Clayton R. Koppes and Gregory Black, "What to Show the World: The Office of War Information and Hollywood, 1942–1945," *The Journal of American History*, Vol. LXIV, No. 1 (June, 1977), pp. 87–105.

10. Koppes and Black, "What to Show the World," p. 89. *The Hollywood Reporter*, Tuesday, June 22, 1943, p. 4.

11. The original *Manual* was written in the summer of 1942 and updated in April of 1943. Nelson Poynter explained the purpose of the Domestic Bureau of Motion Pictures in a letter to Arch Mercey of the Office of War Information, April 29, 1943, Entry 264, Box 1437, RG 208, WNRC. Koppes and Black suggest that the BMP wished to raise Hollywood producers' sights in the article cited in footnote 9 of this chapter.

12. Koppes and Black, "What to Show the World," p. 91.

13. Letter, Mellet to Poynter, December 30, 1942, Mellett Papers, Box 16, FDR Library.

14. Script reviews following the format described abound in the records of the Bureau of Motion Pictures, RG 209, WNRC.

15. See Dorothy B. Jones, "Quantitative Analysis of Motion Picture Content," *Public Opinion Quarterly*, VI (Fall, 1942), pp. 411–27.

16. Marjorie Thorson, *Script Review: "So Proudly We Hail,"* Film Analysis Section, Hollywood Office, Bureau of Motion Pictures, Office of War Information, Entry 264, Box 1433F, RG 208, WNRC.

17. Ibid., p. 2.

18. Letter, Nelson Poynter to Mark Sandrich, October 26, 1942, Entry 264, Box 1433F, RG 208, WNRC.

19. Ibid., pp. 1–2.

20. Ibid., p. 2.

21. Second Review, *Feature Script: "So Proudly We Hail."*

22. Ibid., p. 1.

23. Ibid., p. 1.

24. Ibid., pp. 1–2.

25. Ibid. Also see page 3 of the final review of *So Proudly We Hail*, cited in footnote 28.

26. Letter, Mellett to Poynter, December 30, 1942, Mellett Papers, Box 16, FDR Library, pp. 1–2.

27. Ibid., p. 2.

28. Peg Fenwick, *Feature Viewing: "So Proudly We Hail,"* Film Analysis Section, Hollywood Office, BMP, OWI, Entry 264, Box 1433F, RG 208, WNRC.

29. Ibid., pp. 1–2.

30. Lois Banner noted that nursing became a field dominated by women as early as 1910. *Women in Modern America*, pp. 10–11.

31. For a different evaluation of the efforts of the BMP, read the excellent article by Koppes and Black cited fully in footnote 9 of this chapter.

32. James Agee, *Agee on Film*, p. 52.

33. The characterization of *Air Force* as a "violently masculine" film came from James Agee, *Agee on Film*, p. 28.

34. See the *Script Review* written by Marjorie Thorson of the BMP (Entry 264, Box 1438, RG 208, WNRC) or a similar synopsis entitled *Feature and Serial Analysis: Air Force* written by staff members of the Bureau of Intelligence (Air Force File, Motion Picture Division, Library of Congress).

35. Chapter 4 of this work includes an analysis of *Since You Went Away*.

Conclusion

1. Ernest W. Burgess, "The Effects of the War on the American Family," *American Journal of Sociology*, Vol. 48 (November, 1942), pp. 343–52. Burgess' article may also be read in Keith L. Nelson's *The Impact of War on American Life: The Twentieth Century Experience* (New York, 1971), pp. 134–141.

2. Chafe, *The American Woman*, pp. 195, 246, 147.

3. Ibid., pp. 247–48, 195, 248.

4. Ibid., p. 195. Carl Degler's ideas are explained more fully in his article, "Revolution Without Ideology: The Changing Place of Women in America," in Robert J. Lifton, ed., *The Woman in America* (Boston, 1967), pp. 193–210.

5. Chafe, *American Woman*, p. 245 and chapter 8, "The Paradox of Change." For accounts of the domestic female as the major image in films of the post-war decades, read Rosen's *Popcorn Venus*, pp. 259–365 or Haskell's *From Reverence to Rape*, pp. 231–276. Friedan's *Feminine Mystique* is the basic work on popular heroines in magazine short stories. Also see her article, "Betty Friedan Reviews the Changing Image of Women," for a description of television heroines, p. C-17. Filene discusses Americans' eagerness to return to old patterns following World War II in *Him/Her/Self*, pp. 168–176.

6. Filene, *Him/Her/Self*, pp. 168–176.

7. See Friedan's *Feminine Mystique*.

8. Roosevelt's praise of the family is found in a letter to Mrs. Robert A. Angelo, president of the National Council of Catholic Women, October 17, 1944. President's Personal Files, 8919, Franklin D. Roosevelt's Library, Hyde Park, New York. For recent defenses of women's traditional roles, see Helen Andelin, *Fascinating Womanhood* (Santa Barbara, 1965), and Marabel Morgan, *The Total Woman* (New York, 1973).

9. *A Statistical Portrait of Women in the United States*, Current Population Reports, Special Studies Series P-23, No. 58 (April 1976), Bureau of the Census, United States Department of Commerce.

10. Chafe, *American Woman*, chapters 8 and 9.

Bibliography

Film Research

Motion Picture Division
Library of Congress, Washington, D.C.

Air Force (WB, 1943)

And Now Tomorrow (Paramount, 1944)

Behind the Rising Sun (RKO, 1943)

Bells of St. Mary, The (RKO, 1945)

Best Years of Our Lives, The (MGM, 1946)

Casablanca (WB, 1943)

Claudia (20th Century-Fox, 1943)

Coney Island (20th Century-Fox, 1943)

Cover Girl (Columbia, 1944)

Gilda (Columbia, 1946)

Going My Way (Paramount, 1944)

Guadalcanal Diary (20th Century-Fox, 1943)

Guy Named Joe, A (MGM, 1944)

Heaven Can Wait (20th Century-Fox, 1943)

Here Come the Waves (Paramount, 1945)

Hitler's Children (RKO, 1943)

Incendiary Blonde (Paramount, 1945)

Kid from Brooklyn, The (RKO, 1946)

Killers, The (Universal, 1946)

Lady Takes a Chance, A (RKO, 1943)

Leave Her to Heaven (20th Century-Fox, 1946)

Let's Face It (Paramount, 1943)

Love Thy Neighbor (Paramount, 1941)

Meet Me in St. Louis (MGM, 1944)

Mr. Lucky (RKO, 1943)

Mrs. Miniver (MGM, 1942)

Night and Day (WB, 1946)

Outlaw, The (Howard Hughes, 1946)

Pride of the Yankees, The (RKO, 1942)

Princess and the Pirate, The (RKO, 1944)

Road to Utopia (Paramount, 1946)

Saratoga Trunk (WB, 1946)

Sea Wolf (WB, 1941)

Sergeant York (WB, 1941)

Since You Went Away (Selznick International, 1944)

So Proudly We Hail (Paramount, 1943)

Spellbound (Vanguard Films, 1945)

Sweet Rosie O'Grady (20th Century-Fox, 1943)

Thirty Seconds Over Tokyo (MGM, 1944)

This Is the Army (WB, 1943)

Thrill of a Romance (MGM, 1945)

Tree Grows in Brooklyn, A (20th Century-Fox, 1945)

Valley of Decision, The (MGM, 1945)

Winged Victory (20th Century-Fox, 1944)

Wonder Man (RKO, 1945)

Yankee Doodle Dandy (WB, 1942)

Film Archives
University of California, Los Angeles

Ebb Tide (Paramount, 1937)

Frenchman's Creek (Paramount, 1937)

Gunga Din (RKO, 1939)

Lady in the Dark (Paramount, 1943)

Meet John Doe (WB, 1941)

Rains Came, The (20th Century-Fox, 1939)

Stanley and Livingstone (20th Century-Fox, 1939)

Trail of the Lonesome Pine (Paramount, 1937)

Union Pacific (Paramount, 1939)

Motion Picture Archives
National Archives, Washington, D.C.

March of Time, 1942–1945

Paramount Newsreels, 1941–1945

Special Documentaries with War Content, 1941–1945

United News, 1942–1945

Manuscript Collections

Academy of Motion Pictures Arts and Sciences Archives, Los Angeles.

American Film Institute Archives, Beverly Hills.

Anne Martin Papers, Bancroft Library, University of California, Berkeley.

Bureau of Intelligence, Office of Government Reports Papers. Library of Congress, Washington, D.C.

Bureau of Motion Pictures (Domestic Branch) Papers, Office of War Information Collection, Washington National Records Center, Suitland, Md.

Eleanor Roosevelt Papers, Franklin D. Roosevelt Library, Hyde Park, N.Y.

Franklin Delano Roosevelt Papers, Franklin D. Roosevelt Library, Hyde Park, N.Y.

Library of Congress—Museum of Modern Art Film Preservation Project Papers, Library of Congress, Washington, D.C.

Lowell Mellett Papers, Franklin D. Roosevelt Library, Hyde Park, N.Y.

Motion Picture Feature Film Archives, Library of Congress, Washington, D.C.

Office of War Information Papers, Washington National Records Center, Suitland, Md.

Government Publications

Bertrand, Daniel. *The Motion Picture Industry: A Pattern of Control*. Washington, D.C., 1941.

Bureau of the Census. *The Social and Economic Status of the Black Population in the United States*. Washington, D.C., 1975.

————. *A Statistical Portrait of Women in the United States*. Washington, D.C., 1976.

Bureau of Intelligence, Office of War Information. *Rumors on Manpower*. Washington, D.C., 1942.

Bureau of Motion Pictures. *Evaluation of Motion Pictures*. Washington, D.C., 1942.

————. *Women At War*. Washington, D.C., 1942.

Cochran, Blake. *Films on War and American Policy*. Washington, D.C., 1940.

Office for Emergency Management. *Government Statistics on Women*. Washington, D.C., 1942.

————. *Statements of Private Thought: Leaders on Women and the War*. Washington, D.C., 1942.

Office of Government Reports. *Preliminary Information on Women and the War Effort*. Washington, D.C., July 14, 1942.

————. *Weekly Summary and Analysis of Feature Motion Pictures*. Washington, D.C., 1942–1943.

Office of War Information. "The Bullet That's Going to Kill Hitler." *Win the War Script No. 4*. June 12, 1942.

————. *The Enemy in the Movies*. Washington, D.C., 1942.

————. *Feature Films and OWI Campaigns and Programs*. Washington, D.C., 1943.

————. *War Information Manual*. Washington, D.C., 1942.

————. *Womanpower*. Washington, D.C., February 15, 1944.

War Manpower Commission. *Womanpower: An Appraisal by the Women's Advisory Committee*. Washington, D.C., 1944.

Books

Agee, James. *Agee on Films: Reviews and Comments by James Agee*. New York, 1969.

Alexander, Charles C. *Nationalism in American Thought, 1930–1945*. Chicago, 1969.

Andelin, Helen. *Fascinating Womanhood*. Santa Barbara, Ca., 1965.

Arnheim, Rudolf. *Film As Art*. Berkeley, 1967.

Banner, Lois W. *Women in Modern America: A Brief History*. New York, 1974.

Baxandall, Rosalyn; Gordon, Linda; and Reverby, Susan, eds. *America's Working Women*. New York, 1976.

Baxter, John. *Hollywood in the Thirties*. New York, 1968.

Bayer, William. *The Great Movies*. New York, 1973.

Beck, Warren A., and Clowers, Myles L., eds. *Understanding American History through Fiction*. New York, 1975.

Behlmer, Rudy, ed. *Memo from: David O. Selznick*. New York, 1972.

Bergman, Andrew. *We're in the Money: Depression America and Its Films*. New York, 1971.

Blassingame, John. *The Slave Community: Plantation Life in the Antebellum South*. New York, 1972.

Blum, John M. *V Was for Victory*. New York, 1976.

Blumer, Herbert. *Movies and Conduct*. New York, 1933.

Boulding, Elise. *The Underside of History: A View of Women through Time*. Boulder, Colorado, 1976.

Capra, Frank. *The Name above the Title*. New York, 1971.

Cater, Libby A; Scott, Anne Firor; and Martyna, Wendy, eds. *Women and Men: Changing Roles, Relationships and Perceptions*. Palo Alto, Ca., 1976.

Chafe, William H. *The American Woman: Her Changing Social, Economic and Political Role, 1920–1970*. New York, 1972.

————. *Women and Equality: Changing Patterns in American Culture*. Oxford, 1977.

Coben, Stanley, and Ratner, Lorman, eds. *The Development of an American Culture*. New Jersey, 1970.

Crowther, Bosley. *Movies and Censorship*. New York, 1962.

Daniels, Roger. *The Politics of Prejudice*. New York, 1970.

David, Jane T. "An Investigation of the Image of American Women in Selected American Motion Pictures, 1930–1971." Ph.D. dissertation, New York University, 1975.

Degen, Marie Louise. *The History of the Woman's Peace Party*. Baltimore, 1939.

Deming, Barbara. *Running Away from Myself: A Dream Portrait of America Drawn from the Films of the Forties*. New York, 1969.

Filene, Peter. *Him/Her/Self: Sex Roles in Modern America*. New York, 1976.

Fitzgerald, F. Scott. *The Last Tycoon*. New York, 1941.

Flexner, Eleanor. *Century of Struggle: The Women's Rights Movement in the United States*. New York, 1959.

French, Philip. *The Movie Moguls*. London, 1969.

Friedan, Betty. *The Feminine Mystique*. New York, 1963.

Gilman, Charlotte Perkins. *Women and Economics*. Boston, 1898.

Girdner, Audrie, and Loftis, Anne. *The Great Betrayal*. New York, 1969.

Goodman, Jack, ed. *While You Were Gone: A Report on Wartime Life in the United States*. New York, 1946.

Greenberg, Joel, and Higham, Charles. *Hollywood in the Forties*. London, 1968.

Gregory, Chester. *Women in Defense Work in World War II*. New York, 1974.

Groves, Robert, and Hodge, Alan. *The Long Week-end: A Social History of Great Britain, 1918–1939*. New York, 1963.

Handel, Leo. *Hollywood Looks at Its Audience: A Report of Film Audience Research*. Urbana, 1950.

Haskell, Molly. *From Reverence to Rape: The Treatment of Women in the Movies*. New York, 1973.

Higham, Charles. *The Art of the American Film, 1900–1971*. Garden City, 1973.

Hughes, Robert, ed. *Film: Book Z, Films of Peace and War*. New York, 1962.

Inglis, Ruth A. *Freedom of the Movies*. Chicago, 1947.

Irwin, Inez Haynes. *Up Hill with Banners Flying*. Penobscot, Maine, 1964.

Jacobs, Lewis. *The Rise of the American Film*. New York, 1939.

Jowett, Garth. *Film: The Democratic Art, A Social History of American Film*. Boston, 1976.

————. "The Motion Picture in America, 1894–1936." Ph.D. dissertation, University of Pennsylvania, 1972.

Jones, Ken D., and McClure, Arthur. *Hollywood at War: The American Motion Picture and World War II*. New York, 1973.

Kauffman, Stanley, ed. *American Film Criticism: From the Beginnings to Citizen Kane*. New York, 1972.

Kay, Karyn, and Peary, Gerald. *Women and the Cinema: A Critical Anthology*. New York, 1977.

Kelly, Judith. *Marriage is a Private Affair*. New York, 1941.

Kenney, William. *The Crucial Years, 1940–1945*. New York, 1962.

Kowalski, Rosemary. *Women and Film: A Bibliography*. New Jersey, 1976.

Knight, Arthur. *The Liveliest Art: A Panoramic History of the Movies*. New York, 1957.

Kracauer, Siegfried. *From Caligari to Hitler: A Psychological History of the German Film*. Princeton, 1947.

Kraditor, Aileen S. *The Ideas of the Women Suffrage Movement, 1890–1920*. New York, 1965.

Lash, Joseph P. *Eleanor and Franklin*. New York, 1971.

Lerner, Gerda. *The Woman in American History*. Menlo Park, Ca., 1971.

Levin, Martin, ed. *Hollywood and the Great Fan Magazines*. New York, 1970.

Leyda, Jay. *Films Beget Films: Compilation Films from Propaganda to Drama*. New York, 1964.

Lifton, Robert J., ed. *The Woman in America*. Boston, 1967.

Lingeman, Richard. *Don't You Know There's a War On? The American Home Front, 1941–1945*. New York, 1970.

Lloyd, Charles D. "American Society and Values in World War II from the Publications of the Office of War Information." Ph.D. dissertation, Georgetown University, 1975.

Look editors. *Movie Lot to Beachhead: The Motion Picture Goes to War and Prepares for the Future*. New York, 1945.

Lynch, William. *The Image Industries*. New York, 1959.

MacCann, Richard D. *The People's Films: A Political History of U.S. Government Motion Pictures*. New York, 1973.

McClure, Arthur F., ed. *The Movies: An American Idiom*. New Jersey, 1971.

Mast, Gerald. *A Short History of the Movies*. New York, 1971.

Mellen, Joan. *Women and their Sexuality in the New Film*. New York, 1973.

Mehr, Linda Harris. "Down Off the Pedestal: Some Modern Heroines in Popular Culture, 1890–1917." Ph.D. dissertation, University of California, Los Angeles, 1973.

Michael, Paul, ed. *The American Movies Reference Book, The Sound Era*. New Jersey, 1969.

Monaco, James. *How to Read a Film: The Art, Technology, Language, History and Theory of Film and Media*. Oxford, 1977.

Morgan, Marabel. *Total Joy*. New York, 1976.

————. *The Total Woman*. New York, 1973.

Nye, Russell. *The Unembarrassed Muse: The Popular Arts in America*. New York, 1970.

North, Douglas C. *Growth and Welfare in the American Past: A New Economic History*. New Jersey, 1966.

O'Neill, William L. *Everyone Was Brave: A History of Feminism in America*. Chicago, 1971.

Perrett, Geoffrey. *Days of Sadness, Years of Triumph: The American People, 1939–1945*. Baltimore, 1974.

Ramsaye, Terry, ed. *The International Motion Picture Almanac*. New York, 1942.

Randall, Richard S. *Censorship of the Movies*. Madison, Wis.: 1968.

Rosen, Marjorie. *Popcorn Venus: Women, Movies and the American Dream*. New York, 1973.

Rotha, Paul, and Griffith, Richard, eds. *The Film Till Now*. New York, 1951.

Rupp, Leila J. *Mobilizing Women for War: German and American Propaganda 1939–1945*. New Jersey, 1978.

Schickel, Richard. *Movies: The History of an Art and an Institution*. New York, 1964.

Schillaci, Anthony. *Movies and Morals*. Notre Dame, Ind., 1968.

Shales, Tom, ed. *The American Film Heritage: Impressions from the American Film Institute Archives*. Washington, D.C., 1972.

Shirer, William L. *The Rise and Fall of the Third Reich*. New York, 1960.

Sklar, Robert. *Movie-Made America: A Social History of American Movies*. New York, 1975.

Sochen, June, ed. *The New Feminism in Twentieth Century America*. Lexington, 1971.

Stanton, Elizabeth Cady. *Eighty Years and More*. New York, 1898.

Talbot, Daniel, ed. *Film: An Anthology*. Berkeley, Ca., 1966.

Taylor, A. J. P. *English History 1914–1945*. New York, 1965.

Tebbel, John. *The Media in America*. New York, 1974.

Terkel, Studs. *Hard Times*. New York, 1970.

Time-Life Books. *This Fabulous Century, 1940–1950*. New York, 1969.

Toland, John. *The Rising Sun: The Decline and Fall of the Japanese Empire*. New York, 1970.

Tyler, Parker. *Magic and Myth of Movies*. New York, 1947.

Walker, Alexander. *The Celluloid Sacrifice: Aspects of Sex in the Movies*. New York, 1967.

Warner, W. Lloyd. *American Life: Dream and Reality*. Chicago, 1953.

Weibel, Kathryn. *Mirror, Mirror: Images of Women Reflected in Popular Culture*. Garden City, 1977.

Wolfenstein, Martha, and Leites, Nathan. *Movies: A Psychological Study*. Glencoe, 1950.

Zinsser, William. *Seen Any Good Movies Lately?* New York, 1958.

Zukor, Adolph. *The Public Is Never Wrong*. New York, 1953.

Articles

Banner, Lois W. "On Writing Women's History." *Journal of Interdisciplinary History*, Fall, 1971.

Black, Gregory D., and Koppes, Clayton R. "OWI Goes to the Movies: The Bureau of Intelligence's Criticism of Hollywood, 1942–43." *Prologue, The Journal of the National Archives*, Spring, 1974.

Bourget, Jean-Loup. "Romantic Dramas of the Forties." *Film Comment*, January, February, 1974.

Bradley, LaVerne. "Women at Work." *National Geographic*, August, 1944.

Bromley, Dorothy D. "Women on the Home Front." *Harper's*, July, 1941.

Burgess, Ernest W. "The Effects of the War on the American Family." *American Journal of Sociology*, November, 1942.

Degler, Carl N. "Charlotte Perkins Gilman on the Theory and Practice of Feminism." *American Quarterly*, Spring, 1956.

————. "Revolution without Ideology: The Changing Place of Women in America." Robert J. Lifton, ed. *The Woman in America*, Boston, 1967.

Deming, Barbara. "The Library of Congress Film Project: Exposition of a Method." *The Library of Congress Quarterly Journal of Current Acquisitions*, November, 1944.

Elkin, Frederick. "Value Implications of Popular Films." *Sociology and Social Research*, May/June, 1954.

Farber, Stephen. "The Vanishing Heroine." *Hudson Review*, Winter, 1974–75.

Fearing, Franklin. "Films As History." *Hollywood Quarterly*, 1947.

Friedan, Betty. "Betty Friedan Reviews the Changing Image of Women." Santa Barbara *News-Press*, April 23, 1978.

Gutcheon, Beth. "TV: There's Nothing Wishy-Washy about Soaps." *Ms.*, August, 1974.

Handzo, Stephen. "A Decade of Good Deeds and Wonderful Lives under Capracorn." *Film Comment*, November-December, 1972.

Hareven, Tamera K. "The History of the Family as an Interdisciplinary Field." *Journal of Interdisciplinary History*, Fall, 1971.

Haskell, Molly. "Howard Hawks Masculine Feminine." *Film Comment*, March, April, 1974.

Haynes, Howard. "Movies in the 1950s: Sexism from A to Zapata." *Journal of the University Film Association*, 1974.

Higham, John. "American Intellectual History: A Critical Appraisal." *American Quarterly*, 1961.

Hine, Al. "War Films." *Holiday*, September, 1949.

Hofstadter, Beatrice K. "Popular Culture and the Romantic Heroine." *American Scholar*, Winter, 1960–61.

Houston, Penelope. "The Nature of the Evidence." *Sight and Sound*, Spring, 1967.

Isenberg, Michael T. "A Relationship of Constrained Anxiety: Historians and Film." *History Teacher*, August, 1973.

————. "Toward an Historical Methodology for Film Scholarship." *Rocky Mountain Social Science Journal*, January, 1975.

Jacobs, Lewis. "World War II and the American Film." *Cinema Journal*, Winter, 1967–68.

Jones, Dorothy B. "Hollywood Goes to War." *Nation*, January 27, 1945.

————. "Quantitative Analysis of Motion Picture Content." *Public Opinion Quarterly*, Fall, 1942.

————. "War Films Made in Hollywood, 1942–1944." *Hollywood Quarterly*, October, 1945.

Jones, James. "Phony War Films." *Saturday Evening Post*, March 30, 1963.

Koppes, Clayton R., and Black, Gregory. "What to Show the World: The Office of War Information and Hollywood, 1942–1945." *Journal of American History*, June, 1977.

Larson, Cedric. "The Domestic Motion Picture Work of the Office of War Information." *Hollywood Quarterly*, 1947–1948.

Lerner, Gerda. "New Approaches to the Study of Women in American History." *Journal of Social History* 1969.

McCreary, Eugene. "Film and History: Some Thoughts on Their Interrelationship." *Societas*, Winter, 1971.

McGovern, James R. "The American Woman's Pre-World War I Freedom in Manner and Morals." *Journal of American History*, September, 1968.

Mezerik, A. G. "Getting Rid of the Women." *Atlantic Monthly*, June, 1945.

Price, James. "Smoke-tinted Spectacles: War Films." *London Magazine*, February, 1966.

Putnam, Harold. "The War Against War Movies." *Educational Screen*, May, 1943.

Riesman, David. "The Oral Tradition, the Written Word, and the Screen Image." *Film Culture*, 1956.

Road, Christopher H. "Film As Historical Evidence." Society of Archivists *Journal*, October, 1966.

Robertson, P., and Jones, H. "Housekeeping after the War." *Harper's*, April, 1944.

Rock, Gail. "Same Time, Same Station, Same Sexism." *Ms.*, December, 1973.

Rollins, Peter C. "Victory At Sea: Cold War Epic." *Journal of Popular Culture*, Winter, 1973.

Rosenzweig, Sidney. "The Dark Night of the Screen: Message and Melodrama in the American Movie." *American Quarterly*, March, 1975.

Ryan, Mary P. "The Projection of a New Womanhood: The Movie Moderns in the 1920s." Friedman, Jean E. and Shade, William G., eds. *Our American Sisters: Women in American Life and Thought*. Boston, 1976.

Schlesinger, Arthur, Jr. "When the Movies Really Counted." *Show*, April, 1963.

Skotheim, Robert. "The Writing of American Histories of Ideas: Two Traditions in the XXth Century." *Journal of the History of Ideas*, 1964.

Stults, Taylor. "World War II Films As Propaganda." *Films and History*, May, 1972.

Thompson, Dorothy. "Will Women's Way Rule Tomorrow's World?" *Library*, 1941.

Tobias, Sheila. "Finding Women's History." *Ms.*, November, 1972.

Trecker, Janice Law. "The Suffrage Prisoners." *American Scholar*, Summer, 1972.

Valentine, E. R. "Odyssey of the Army Wife." *New York Times Magazine*, March 5, 1944.

Weinberg, David. "The 'Socially Acceptable' Immigrant Minority Group: The Image of the Jew in American Popular Films." *North Dakota Quarterly*, Autumn, 1972.

Wilkinson, Virginia S. "From Housewife to Shipfitter." *Harper's*, September, 1943.

Young, Colin. "Nobody Dies: Shades of Patriotism in the Hollywood War and 'Anti-War' Film." *Film: Book 2*. Robert Hughes, ed. New York, 1962.

Zangrando, Joanna S. "Women's Studies in the United States: Approaching Reality." *American Studies International*, Autumn, 1975.

Articles by Magazine Title

Boxoffice Barometer
All issues, 1942–1945.

Film and History
1973–1975.

Hollywood Reporter
1942–1945.

Life
"Hitler's Children," February 1, 1943;
"Sergeant York," July 14, 1941;
"Since You Went Away," July 24, 1944.

New Republic
Farber, Manny. "Movies in Wartime," January 3, 1944.
————. "Mrs. Miniver," June 15, 1942.
————. "Sergeant York," September 29, 1941.
————. "Since You Went Away," July 17, 1944.

New Yorker
Lardner, David. "Behind the Rising Sun," October 16, 1943.
————. "Hitler's Children," March 6, 1943.
————. "Since You Went Away," July 29, 1944.
Mosher, John. "Meet John Doe," March 22, 1941.
————. "Sergeant York," July 5, 1941.

Newsweek
"Behind the Rising Sun," August 23, 1943.
"Meet John Doe," March 24, 1941.
"Mrs. Miniver," June 15, 1942.
"Sergeant York," July 4, 1941.
"Since You Went Away," July 10, 1944.

Time
Agee, James. "Since You Went Away," July 17, 1944.
"Behind the Rising Sun," August 7, 1943.
"Casablanca," November 30, 1942.
"Meet John Doe," March 3, 1941.
"Mrs. Miniver," June 29, 1942.
"Sergeant York," August 4, 1941.

Index